John Stevens

Fehlerfrei Englisch

Ein Übungsbuch zum Verlernen typischer Fehler

Wortschatz
Grammatik
Präpositionen

Max Hueber Verlag

Dieses Werk folgt der seit dem 1. August 1998 gültigen Rechtschreibreform.

5. 4. 3. | Die letzten Ziffern
2007 06 05 04 03 | bezeichnen Zahl und Jahr des Druckes.
Alle Drucke dieser Auflage können, da unverändert, nebeneinander benutzt werden.
1. Auflage

Redaktion: Elisabeth Dorner, Berlin; Jürgen Frank, München
Umschlaggestaltung: Parzhuber & Partner, München
Satz: Design-Typo-Print GmbH, Ismaning
Druck und Bindung: Druckhaus am Kitzenmarkt, Augsburg
Printed in Germany
ISBN 3-19-002699-8

Vorwort

„Ich möchte mein Englisch verbessern."

„Ich mache beim Englischsprechen immer wieder dieselben typisch deutschen Fehler."

„Meine Muttersprache stellt mir immer wieder eine Falle, wenn ich Englisch rede, und ich tappe immer wieder hinein."

„Bestimmte Sachverhalte werden im Deutschen und im Englischen ganz ähnlich ausgedrückt, andere aber völlig unterschiedlich, und das führt immer wieder zu Fehlern. Ich möchte gezielt an diesen Fehlerquellen arbeiten, um sie in Zukunft zu vermeiden."

Erkennen Sie sich in der einen oder anderen Aussage wieder? Wenn ja, dann halten Sie das richtige Buch in der Hand, denn es trainiert das Verlernen typisch deutscher Fehler in den drei wichtigen Bereichen Wortschatz, Grammatik und beim Gebrauch der Präpositionen. Und weil alle guten Dinge drei sind, können Sie auch auf dreierlei Art und Weise mit dem Buch arbeiten: Sie können damit a) lernen, b) üben und c) Ihren Lernerfolg in Tests kontrollieren.

Auf der nächsten Seite machen wir Ihnen Vorschläge, wie Sie am besten vorgehen.

1. Sie wählen (s. Inhaltsverzeichnis S. 5–7) einen Bereich aus, den Sie gezielt bearbeiten möchten. Oder Sie entscheiden sich dafür, das gesamte Buch nach und nach von vorne bis hinten systematisch durchzuarbeiten.
2. Sie lesen die Hinweise und Erklärungen zu Beginn jedes Kapitels bzw. Stichworts und achten dabei besonders auf die Informationen, die mit dem Pfeil gekennzeichnet sind. Diese verweisen auf die jeweilige Fehlerquelle.
3. Sie bearbeiten die Übungssätze, kontrollieren dann anschließend Ihre Lösungen durch Vergleich mit dem (bis dahin sinnvollerweise abgedeckten) Schlüssel, den Sie auf jeder Doppelseite unten rechts finden.
4. Sie markieren ggf. die Übungssätze, die noch nicht korrekt gelöst wurden, um sie zu einem späteren Zeitpunkt zu wiederholen.
5. Nach Abschluss eines Kapitels bearbeiten Sie zur Erfolgskontrolle den dazugehörigen Test.

Sie werden merken, wie die typischen Fehler nach und nach aus Ihrem Englisch verschwinden und Sie sich Ihrem Ziel immer mehr nähern: Fehlerfrei Englisch.

Good luck, viel Erfolg!

Inhaltsverzeichnis

3 Präpositionen

Heißt es *at, on* oder etwa *to*?

1 Wortschatz

1.1 Nur so weit, aber nicht weiter!

Deutsch-englische Wortpaare, deren Bedeutung sich nur teilweise deckt

Ergänzen Sie.

allein – *alone*

→	• allein (ohne Anwesenheit anderer, einsam) = *alone* • allein (ohne fremde Hilfe) = *on my/his/... own, by my-/him-/...self*

1 Sie war nicht **allein**. Sie lag auf dem Sofa mit – ach, das sage ich besser nicht.
She was not ______________________ . She was lying on the sofa with – oh, I'd better not say.

2 Diesen Schrank habe ich **allein** gebaut. – Genauso sieht er auch aus!
I built this cupboard ______________________ . – That's just what it looks like.

3 Sein Arm ist gebrochen. Er kann sich nicht **allein** anziehen.
His arm is broken. He can't get dressed ______________________ .

beißen – *bite*

→	• beißen (mit den Zähnen) = *bite* • beißen (Farben) = *clash*

1 So kannst du nicht gehen. Die Krawatte und das Hemd **beißen** sich furchtbar. Du siehst unmöglich aus.
You can't go like that. The tie and the shirt ______________________ terribly. You look awful.

2 In der Zeitungsüberschrift stand „Mann **beißt** Hund".
In the newspaper headline it said "Man ______________________ dog".

3 Ich finde, der Hintergrund und die rote Schrift **beißen** sich.
I think the background and the red text ______________________ .

bringen – *bring*

→ • bringen (herbringen) = *bring*
• bringen (hinbringen, wegbringen) = *take*
(jeweils von dort aus, wo sich der Sprecher effektiv oder gedanklich befindet)
• bringen (ins Bett bringen) = *put (to bed)*

1 Wenn ich das nächste Mal hinfahre, **bringe** ich ihnen die Fotos mit.
When I go there next time, I'll ______________________ *them the photos.*

2 **Bringst** du mich zum Bahnhof?
Will you ______________________ *me to the station?*

3 Wer **bringt** die Kinder **ins Bett**?
Who is going to ______________________ *the children to bed?*

4 Ihr braucht kein Bettzeug mitzu**bringen**, wir haben genug.
You don't need to ______________________ *any bedding, we've got enough.*

5 Ich **bringe** dich nach Hause. Das liegt auf meinem Weg.
I'll ______________________ *you home. It's on my way.*

Brot – *bread*

→ • Brot (geschnitten oder als Laib) = *bread*
• Brot (belegtes, Klapp-) = *sandwich*

1 Wie viele **Brote** soll ich dir einpacken?
How many ______________________ *shall I pack you?*

2 Ein Käse**brot** oder ein Schinken**brot**?
A cheese ______________________ *or a ham* ______________________ *?*

allein [1]alone [2]on my own / by myself [3]on his own / by himself
beißen [1]clash [2]bites [3]clash **bringen** [1]take [2]take [3]put [4]bring [5]take
Brot [1]sandwiches [2]sandwich, sandwich

delikat – *delicate*

> ➔ • delikat (heikel) = *delicate*
> • delikat (wohlschmeckend) = *delicious*

1 Das ist eine sehr **delikate** Angelegenheit. Sag du es ihr lieber.
This is a very ______________________ *matter. It's better if you tell her.*

2 Mhm. Die Soße ist richtig **delikat**.
Mhm. The sauce is really ______________________ .

dick – *thick*

> ➔ • dick (mit überdurchschnittlichem Durchmesser – bei Sachen) = *thick*
> • dick (beleibt) = *fat*
> • dick (üppig in Bezug auf Geld) = *big fat*
> • dick (Fehler) = *big*

1 Sie fährt ein **dickes** Auto. Als Broker hat sie bestimmt ein **dickes** Gehalt.
She drives a ______________________ *car. As a broker I bet she has a* ______________________ *salary.*

2 Wir haben einen **dicken** Fehler gemacht.
We've made a ______________________ *mistake.*

3 Wie **dick** sind die Mauern, weißt du das?
How ______________________ *are the walls, do you know?*

4 Er ist so **dick**, er kann die eigenen Füße nicht mehr sehen.
He's so ______________________*, he can't see his own feet any more.*

5 Torten und Kuchen **machen dick**.
Gateaus and cakes make you ______________________ .

Übrigens: ein dicker Kuss = *a* **big** *kiss*; dicke Freunde = **close** *friends*; eine dicke Rechnung = *a* **hefty** *bill*

falsch – *false*

➔	• falsch (unwahr, unecht) = *false* • falsch (fehlerhaft, nicht korrekt) = *wrong*

1 Sind diese Sätze richtig oder **falsch**?
Are these sentences right or ____________________________ ?

2 Wir sind zur **falschen** Zeit gekommen.
We've come at the ____________________________ time.

3 Der Mann gab absichtlich eine **falsche** Adresse an.
The man deliberately gave a ____________________________ address.

4 Er fuhr auf der **falschen** Straßenseite.
He was driving on the ____________________________ side of the road.

5 Im Lebenslauf gab sie ein **falsches** Geburtsdatum an.
In her CV she gave a ____________________________ date of birth.

Fotografie – *photography*

➔	• Fotografie (Tätigkeit, Hobby) = *photography* • Fotografie (Foto, Bild) = *photograph*

1 Seine besten **Fotografien** sind in der Ausstellung zu sehen.
His best ____________________________ can be seen in the exhibition.

2 **Fotografie** war seine große Leidenschaft.
____________________________ was his great love.

delikat [1]delicate [2]delicious **dick** [1]big fat, big fat [2]big [3]thick [4]fat [5]fat **falsch** [1]wrong [2]wrong [3]false [4]wrong [5]false **Fotografie** [1]photographs [2]Photography

frisch – *fresh*

→ • frisch (kühl/kalt, rein – Eigenschaft von etwas) = *fresh* • frisch (kühl/kalt – Empfinden von Menschen) = *cool/cold*

1 Es wehte eine **frische** Brise.
A ____________________ breeze was blowing.

2 Mir ist es etwas zu **frisch** ohne Pullover.
It's a bit too ____________________ for me without a pullover.

3 Ich brauche etwas **frische** Luft. Ich gehe zehn Minuten spazieren.
I need some ____________________ air. I'm going for a ten-minute walk.

Glas – *glass*

→ • Glas (Material, Trinkgefäß, Getränk) = *glass* • Glas (Aufbewahrungsgefäß mit Deckel) = *jar*

1 ein **Glas** Honig / Oliven / Marmelade
a ____________________ of honey/olives/jam

2 Nimm doch ein anderes **Glas** für den Rotwein.
Let's have a different ____________________ for the red wine.

golden – *golden*

→ • golden (im übertragenen Sinne) = *golden* • golden (sachlich: „aus dem Material Gold“, „goldfarben“) = *gold*

1 Eine **goldene** Uhr und **goldene** Ohrringe im Wert von mehr als $ 5000 wurden entwendet.
A ____________________ watch and ____________________ earrings worth more than $5000 were stolen.

2 Er hat eine **goldene** Regel verletzt, er hat zuerst gesprochen.
He broke a ______________________ *rule by speaking first.*

3 Sie feiern nächste Woche ihre **Gold**hochzeit.
They're celebrating their ______________________ *wedding next week.*

grillen – ***grill***

> ➔ • grillen (Kochvorgang drinnen) = *grill*
> • grillen (Kochvorgang draußen) = *barbecue*
> • grillen (Gesamtvorgang draußen – sitzen, kochen, essen) = *have a barbecue*

1 Wollen wir nicht heute Abend **grillen**? Es ist so schön draußen.
Why don't we ______________________ *this evening? It's so nice outside.*

2 Wir haben einen Herd mit Grill, weil wir Fleisch oft **grillen** statt braten.
We have a stove with a grill because we often ______________________ *meat instead of frying it.*

3 Auf diesem wackligen Ding kannst du doch nicht Steaks für 40 Gäste **grillen**.
You can't ______________________ *steaks for 40 guests on this wobbly thing.*

frisch [1]fresh [2]cool / cold [3]fresh **Glas** [1]jar [2]glass **golden** [1]gold, gold [2]golden [3]golden **grillen** [1]have a barbecue [2]grill [3]barbecue

Gymnastik – *gymnastics*

→
- Gymnastik (Turnen als Wettkampfdisziplin mit Turngeräten) = *gymnastics*
- Gymnastik (private Freiübungen) = *exercises*

1 Morgens wenn ich aufstehe, mache ich zuallererst meine **Gymnastik.**
In the morning when I get up the first thing I do is my
_______________ .

2 **Gymnastik** ist doch eine olympische Disziplin, oder?
_______________ *is an Olympic discipline, isn't it?*

Haus – *house*

→
- Haus (Wohnhaus für 1–2 Parteien) = *house*
- Haus (Gebäude) = *building*
- Haus (Firmenräume) = *office*

1 Hohe **Häuser** säumten den Platz.
Tall _______________ *lined the square.*

2 Der Verkaufsleiter ist diese Woche **außer Haus**.
The sales manager is out of the _______________ *this week.*

3 Unsere Wohnung geben wir auf – wir haben ein **Haus** draußen im Grünen gemietet.
We're giving up our flat. We've rented a _______________ *out in the country.*

helfen – *help*

→ • helfen (behilflich sein) = *help*
• helfen gegen (Arzneimittel usw.) = *be good for*
• nichts helfen (aussichtslos sein) = *be no good*

1 Kamillentee **hilft gegen** Bauchschmerzen.
Camomile tea ______________________ *stomach-aches.*

2 Georg wird uns beim Umzug **helfen**.
George will ______________________ *us with the move.*

3 **Es hilft alles nichts**. Wir müssen bezahlen.
______________________ *. We'll have to pay up.*

Karte – *card*

→ • Karte (zum Schreiben; Spielkarte; bei Fußballfoul) = *card*
• Karte (Speisekarte) = *menu*
• Karte (Eintritts-, Fahrkarte) = *ticket*
• Karte (Landkarte) = *map*

1 Sind noch **Karten** für Dienstagabend da?
Have you still got ______________________ *for Tuesday evening?*

2 Der Tourist sagte: „Ich finde diesen Ort *Umleitung* nicht auf der **Karte**."
The tourist said, "I can't find this place Umleitung *on the*
______________________ *."*

3 Wollen wir mal ein **Karten**spiel machen?
Shall we have a game of ______________________ *?*

4 Herr Ober! Können wir bitte noch mal die **Karte** haben?
Waiter. Can we have the ______________________ *again, please.*

Gymnastik 1exercises 2Gymnastics **Haus** 1buildings 2office 3house
helfen 1is good for 2help 3It's no good **Karte** 1tickets 2map 3cards 4menu

kochen – *cook*

➔
- kochen (Essen zubereiten, die Fähigkeit dazu) = *cook*
- kochen (sieden, Wasser zum Siedepunkt bringen, Essen in kochendem Wasser kochen im Gegensatz zu einer anderen Zubereitungsart) = *boil*
- kochen (Tee, Kaffee, Suppe) = *make*

1 Möchten Sie ein **gekochtes** Ei?
Would you like a ______________________ *egg?*

2 Es gibt immer noch Männer, die nicht **kochen** können.
There are still men who can't ______________________ .

3 Wird das Gemüse **gekocht** oder gebraten?
Do you ______________________ *the vegetables or fry them?*

4 Wer **hat** die Suppe **gekocht**? Sie ist ja völlig versalzen.
Who ______________________ *the soup? There's far too much salt in it.*

5 Das Wasser **kocht**. Soll ich den Tee machen?
The water's ______________________ *. Shall I make the tea?*

6 Wie **kocht** man dieses Gemüse?
How do you ______________________ *these vegetables?*

7 Wir machen mal kurz Pause. Ich **koche** frischen Kaffee.
We'll take a short break. I'll ______________________ *some fresh coffee.*

Komma – *comma*

➔
- Komma (Zeichensetzung in Text) = *comma*
- Komma (in Dezimalzahlen) = *point*

1 Wir haben 6,2% (sechs **Komma** zwei Prozent) mehr verkauft als im Vorjahr.
We've sold 6.2% (six ______________________ *two per cent) more than in the previous year.*

2 Der Mann kann nicht schreiben. Wo sind die **Kommas** in diesem Text?
The man can't write. Where are the ____________________ *in this text?*

kommen – *come*

➔	• kommen (herkommen) = *come* • kommen (hinkommen) = *get* • kommen (hingehören) = *go* • kommen lassen = *send for*

1 Die Adresse **kommt** in die obere rechte Ecke.
The address ____________________ *in the top right-hand corner.*

2 Heute Abend habe ich keine Lust zu kochen. Ich **lasse** Pizza **kommen**.
I don't fancy cooking this evening. I'll ____________________ *pizza.*

3 Wie **komme** ich zum Bahnhof? Das Taxi müsste schon längst da sein.
How am I going to ____________________ *to the station? The taxi should have been here ages ago.*

4 Wo ist euer Auto? – Wir **sind** dieses Mal mit dem Bus **gekommen**.
Where's your car? – We ____________________ *by bus this time.*

5 Sie hat über 40 Fieber. Wir müssen den Arzt **kommen lassen**.
She's got a temperature of over 40. We'll have to ____________________ *the doctor.*

6 Wo **kommen** diese Tassen **hin**? – In den Schrank über der Spüle.
Where do these cups ____________________ *? – In the cupboard over the sink.*

kochen [1]boiled [2]cook [3]boil [4]made [5]boiling [6]cook [7]make **Komma** [1]point [2]commas **kommen** [1]goes [2]send for [3]get [4]came [5]send for [6] go

Küche – *kitchen*

→	• Küche (Raum) = *kitchen* • Küche (Essen, Kochkunst) = *cuisine*

1 Die englische **Küche** ist besser als ihr Ruf.
English ______________ *is better than people think.*

2 In der neuen Wohnung haben wir eine große **Küche**.
In the new flat we have a big ______________.

3 In der mediterranen **Küche** werden Fisch, Olivenöl und Knoblauch verwendet.
Fish, olive oil and garlic are used in Mediterranean ______________.

leihen – *lend*

→	• leihen (an jemanden) = *lend* • leihen (von jemandem) = *borrow*

1 Vielleicht können wir ein Zelt von jemandem **leihen**, statt eins zu kaufen.
Maybe we can ______________ *a tent from someone, instead of buying one.*

2 Ich **habe** ihm mal Geld **geliehen**, er hat es aber nie zurückgezahlt.
I once ______________ *him some money, but he never paid it back.*

3 Vorsichtig, das ist nicht meins. Ich **habe** es **geliehen**.
Careful, that's not mine. I've ______________ *it.*

lernen – *learn*

➔ • lernen (generell) = *learn*
• lernen (für die Schule lernen, Hausaufgaben machen, arbeiten) = *study*

1 Er **lernt** es wohl nie.
He'll never _________________________, will he?

2 Tina ist in ihrem Zimmer und **lernt**.
Tina's in her room _________________________ing.

3 Tim **lernt** für die Mathearbeit morgen.
Tim is _________________________ing for the maths test tomorrow.

4 Sie ist gut, sie **lernt** schnell.
She's good, she _________________________ fast.

Maschine – *machine*

➔ • Maschine (Gerät) = *machine*
• Maschine (Flugzeug) = *plane*
• Maschine (Antriebsmotor) = *engine*

1 Die **Maschine** aus London ist verspätet.
The _________________________ from London is delayed.

2 Unsere Wasch**maschine** ist kaputt.
Our washing _________________________ is broken.

3 Ich fahre das Modell mit der 1,8-Liter-Diesel**maschine**.
I drive the model with the 1.8-litre diesel _________________________.

Küche 1cuisine 2kitchen 3cuisine **leihen** 1borrow 2lent 3borrowed **lernen** 1learn 2studying 3studying 4learns **Maschine** 1plane 2machine 3engine

meinen – *mean*

➔	• meinen (im Sinn haben, sagen wollen) = *mean* • meinen (glauben) = *think*

1 Entschuldigung. Ich **habe** das nicht so **gemeint**.
Sorry. I didn't ____________________ *it like that.*

2 Ich weiß, du **hast** es gut **gemeint**.
I know, you ____________________ *well.*

3 Was **meinen** Sie mit „bald"?
What do you ____________________ *by "soon"?*

4 Ich **meine**, dass es schon zu spät ist.
I ____________________ *it's already too late.*

5 Was **meinst** du? – Ich **meine** das auch.
What do you ____________________ *?*
– I ____________________ *so, too.*

6 Er **hat** dich **gemeint**, nicht mich.
He ____________________ *you, not me.*

Menü – *menu*

➔	• Menü (Computermenü) = *menu* • Menü (feste Speisenfolge) = *special/set lunch/set meal*

1 Ich nehme das **Menü** und ein Glas Rotwein.
I'll have the ____________________ *and a glass of red wine.*

2 Mach das Drucker**menü** auf und klicke auf OK.
Open the printer ____________________ *and click on OK.*

Beachten Sie: Englisch *menu* bedeutet im Restaurant nicht „Menü", sondern „Speisekarte": *Waiter, can you bring us the menu again, please?*

Motor – *motor*

➔	• Motor (eines kleineren Geräts) = *motor* • Motor (Antriebsaggregat von Auto, Bus, Flugzeug, Boot, Schiff) = *engine*

1 Das Auto ist dann stehen geblieben. Es war irgendwas am **Motor**.
Then the car broke down. There was something wrong with the ____________________ .

2 Ich fuhr hinter einem Bus mit einem stinkenden Diesel**motor** her.
I drove along behind a bus with a stinking diesel ____________________ .

3 Er ist ein richtiger Bastler. Er hat den **Motor** eines alten Staubsaugers benutzt.
He's a real handyman. He used the ____________________ *of an old vacuum cleaner.*

nächste(r/s) – *next*

➔	• nächste(r/s) (zeitlich, räumlich nächstfolgend) = *next* • nächste(r/s) (räumlich am nächsten, nächstgelegen) = *nearest*

1 Das **nächste** Mal fahren wir lieber mit dem Zug.
____________________ *time it would be better to go by train.*

2 Wo ist die **nächste** Bank?
Where's the ____________________ *bank?*

3 Das **nächste** gute Hotel ist ungefähr einen Kilometer von hier.
The ____________________ *good hotel is about a kilometre from here.*

4 Wer wohnt **am nächsten**?
Who lives ____________________ ?

meinen [1]mean [2]meant [3]mean [4]think [5]think, think [6]meant
Menü [1]special / set lunch / set meal [2]menu **Motor** [1]engine [2]engine [3]motor **nächste(r/s)** [1]Next [2]nearest [3]nearest [4]nearest

Natur – *nature*

→	• Natur (natürliche Welt der Pflanzen, Tiere usw.) = *nature* • die freie Natur = *the open air, the countryside*

1 Großstadtkinder wissen heute oft wenig von der **Natur**.
City children today often know little about ______________________.

2 Am Wochenende bin ich gern in der **Natur**.
At the weekend I like to be in the ______________________.

neueste(r/s) – *newest*

→	• neueste(r/s) (Gegenteil von „älteste[r/s]") = *newest* • neueste(r/s) (bisher letzte[r/s] in einer Reihe) = *latest*

1 Haben Sie die **neuesten** Nachrichten aus LA gehört?
Have you heard the ______________________ *news from LA?*

2 Ich hab's in der **neuesten** Ausgabe der *Times* gelesen.
I read it in the ______________________ *edition of the* Times.

3 Du musst ein Bombengehalt haben. Du fährst immer das aller**neueste** Modell.
You must have a tremendous salary. You always drive the very ______________________ *model.*

null – *nil*

→	• null (Punkte-/Torezählung beim Sport, außer beim Tennis) = *nil* • null (in Temperaturangaben) = *zero* • null (in Dezimalzahlen) = *nought, zero* • null (in Telefon- und Kontonummern) = *oh, zero*

1 Es sind 8 Grad unter **null**.
It's 8 degrees below ______________________.

2 5,04% = fünf Komma **null** 4 Prozent.
5.04% = five point ____________________ four per cent

3 Die Kontonummer lautet 131430(= **null**)2768.
The account number is 131430(= ____________________)2768.

4 Die deutsche Fußballmanschaft hat vier zu **null** gewonnen.
The German football team won four ____________________.

5 Meine Telefonnummer ist 4014 (vier **null** eins vier).
My phone number is 4014 (four ____________________ one four).

Ofen – *oven*

→ • Ofen (Backofen im Herd) = *oven*
• Ofen (zum Heizen) = 1. *stove* (groß, schwer für Holz, Kohle usw.), 2. *heater* (klein, elektrisch betrieben)

1 Sie haben so einen skandinavischen gusseisernen **Ofen**.
They've got one of those Scandinavian cast-iron ____________________s.

2 Wir brauchen einen kleinen **Ofen** für das Badezimmer.
We need a little ____________________ for the bathroom.

3 Backen Sie die Pizza im **Ofen** bei 200°.
Bake the pizza in the ____________________ at 200°.

Natur [1]nature [2]open air / countryside **neueste(r/s)** [1]latest [2]latest [3]latest
null [1]zero [2]nought/zero [3]oh/zero [4]nil [5]oh/zero **Ofen** [1]stove [2]heater [3]oven

Paar – *pair*

→ • Paar (zwei zusammengehörige Dinge, Tiere) = *pair* [Faustregel]
• Paar (zwei zusammengehörige Personen) = *couple* [Faustregel]
• ein paar (einige) = *a couple (of)*

1 Welches **Paar** tanzt am besten?
Which ______________________ *is dancing best?*

2 Tina und Gerd sind ein interessantes **Paar**.
Tina and Gerd are an interesting ______________________.

3 Sie bleiben **ein paar** Tage dort.
They're staying there ______________________ *days.*

4 Ich brauche ein neues **Paar** Schuhe.
I need a new ______________________ *of shoes.*

Pause – *pause*

→ • Pause (kurze Unterbrechung von wenigen Sekunden) = *pause*
• Pause (Erholungspause, Unterbrechung von einigen Minuten) = *break*

1 Ich brauche eine Kaffee**pause**.
I need a coffee ______________________ .

2 Wann machen wir eine **Pause**? Wir arbeiten nonstop seit drei Stunden.
When are we going to have a ______________________*? We've been working non-stop for three hours now.*

3 Es gab eine kurze **Pause**, als er umblätterte.
There was a short ______________________ *when he turned the page.*

4 Es tut mir Leid. Er ist gerade in der Mittags**pause**.
I'm sorry. He's just having his lunch ______________________ .

Politik – *politics*

> ➔ • Politik (politisches Leben / Geschehen allgemein, Staatskunst) = *politics*
> • Politik (Einstellung / Vorhaben / Handlungsweise in bestimmten Bereichen) = *policy*

1 Die Wirtschafts**politik** dieser Regierung ist miserabel.
This government's economic ___________ *is dreadful.*

2 Die Ministerin hatte einigen Erfolg mit dieser neuen **Politik**.
The minister had a certain amount of success with the new ___________ .

3 Die **Politik** interessiert mich wenig.
I'm not very interested in ___________ .

Programm – *program, programme*

> ➔ • Programm (Plan) = *programme* (GB) / *program* (USA)
> • Programm (Computerprogramm) = *program* (GB & USA)
> • Programm (Fernsehkanal) = *channel*

1 Welches **Programm** bringt die besten Musiksendungen?
Which ___________ *has the best music programmes?*

2 Welches Programm verwenden Sie? – Microsoft Word.
Which ___________ *do you use? – Microsoft Word.*

3 Das **Programm** für die holländische Delegation steht.
The ___________ *for the Dutch delegation is ready.*

Paar [1]couple [2]couple [3]a couple of [4]pair **Pause** [1]break [2]break [3]pause [4]break **Politik** [1]policy [2]policy [3]politics **Programm** [1]channel [2]program [3]programme / program

rauben – ***rob***

→ • rauben (einer Person/Bank etwas nehmen) = *rob* • rauben (etwas rauben) = *steal*

1 Er **hat** mich mit einem Messer bedroht und **ausgeraubt**.
He threatened me with a knife and ______________________ *me.*

2 Die Bande **hat** fünf Banken **ausgeraubt**.
The gang have ______________________ *five banks.*

3 Die Einbrecher **haben** Juwelen im Wert von über $10.000 **geraubt**.
The burglars ______________________ *jewellery worth over $10,000.*

Salat – ***salad***

→ • Salat (angemacht als Gericht/Beilage) = *salad* • Salat (als Pflanze/Blätter, Kopfsalat) = *lettuce*

1 Es ist so heiß. Ich esse nur einen **Salat**.
It's so hot. I'll just have a ______________________ .

2 Kannst du bitte einen schönen **Salat** kaufen, wenn du auf den Markt gehst?
Can you buy a nice ______________________ *when you go to the market, please?*

3 Hast du den **Salat** schon gewaschen?
Have you washed the ______________________ *yet?*

scharf – *sharp*

➔ • scharf (Messer, Frost) = *sharp* • scharf (Essen = sehr würzig) = *spicy, hot* • nicht scharf (Foto) = *blurred, fuzzy, out of focus*

1 Schade, dass der Hintergrund nicht **scharf** ist.
A pity the background is ______________________ .

2 Das Essen war so **scharf**, ich kam mir vor wie ein Feuerschlucker.
The food was so ______________________ *I felt like a fire-eater.*

3 Schnell, ich brauche ein **scharfes** Messer.
Quick, I need a ______________________ *knife.*

Schiff – *ship*

➔ • Schiff (groß, auf dem Meer) = *ship* • Schiff (auf Binnengewässern; Fährschiff) = *boat*

1 Wir haben eine **Schiff**sfahrt auf dem See gemacht.
We went on a ______________________ *trip on the lake.*

2 Wie lang braucht ein **Schiff** heutzutage von Europa nach Amerika?
How long does a ______________________ *take to get from Europe to America nowadays?*

3 Fahren Sie mit dem **Schiff** von Calais nach Dover oder durch den Kanaltunnel?
Are you going from Calais to Dover by ______________________ *or through the Channel Tunnel?*

rauben 1robbed 2robbed 3stole **Salat** 1salad 2lettuce 3lettuce **scharf** 1blurred/fuzzy/out of focus 2spicy/hot 3sharp **Schiff** 1boat 2ship 3boat

Schwester – *sister*

→	• Schwester (Familienangehörige) = *sister* • Schwester (Krankenschwester) = *nurse*

1 **Schwester**, kann ich bitte noch ein Kopfkissen haben?
________________________, can I have another pillow, please?

2 Meine **Schwester** Ann ist zwei Jahre älter als ich.
My ________________________ Ann is two years older than me.

3 Die **Schwestern** sind sehr hilfsbereit.
The ________________________ are very helpful.

Soße – *sauce*

→	• Soße (generell) = *sauce* • Soße (Bratensoße) = *gravy* • Soße (Salatsoße) = *dressing*

1 Soll ich die [Braten-]**Soße** über die Kartoffeln tun?
Shall I put the ________________________ over the potatoes?

2 Haben wir noch Soja**soße** im Vorratskeller?
Have we got any soy ________________________ left in the cellar?

3 Eis mit Schokoladen**soße**! Lecker!
Ice-cream and chocolate ________________________! Lovely!

4 Ich mache die [Salat-]**Soße** wie immer mit Öl und Essig.
I'll make the ________________________ with oil and vinegar as usual.

Technik – *technique*

→	• Technik (Methode, Arbeitsweise) = *technique* • Technik (Wissenschaft, Technologie) = *technology*

1 Die ganze Welt der **Technik** unter einem Dach.
The whole world of ____________________ *under one roof.*

2 Die **Technik** entwickelt sich mit rasenden Schritten.
____________________ *is developing in leaps and bounds.*

3 Welche **Technik** hat der Maler benutzt?
Which ____________________ *did the painter use?*

4 Diese **Technik** erfordert viel Übung.
This ____________________ *needs a lot of practice.*

Unterhemd, Weste – *undershirt, vest*

→	• Unterhemd = *undershirt* (in USA), *vest* (in GB) • Weste = *vest* (in USA), *waistcoat* (in GB)

1 Er trug eine knallrote **Weste** unter der Jacke.
He was wearing a bright red ____________________ *(USA)/*
____________________ *(GB) under his jacket.*

2 Er trug ein knallrotes **Unterhemd** unter einem weißen Hemd.
He was wearing a bright red ____________________ *(USA)/*
____________________ *(GB) under a white shirt.*

Schwester [1]Nurse [2]sister [3]nurses **Soße** [1]gravy [2]sauce [3]sauce [4]dressing
Technik [1]technology [2]Technology [3]technique [4]technique
Unterhemd [1]vest, waistcoat [2]undershirt, vest

vergessen – *forget*

➔ • vergessen (Gegenteil von „daran denken, sich erinnern“) = *forget*
• vergessen (liegen lassen) = 1. *leave* (+ Ortsbezeichnung)
2. *leave behind/forget*
(wenn kein Ort genannt wird)

1 Diesen Tag werde ich nie **vergessen**.
I'll never ____________________ *this day.*

2 Ich habe mein Portemonnaie zu Hause **vergessen**.
I've ____________________ *my wallet at home.*

3 Ich darf den Termin heute Nachmittag nicht **vergessen**.
I mustn't ____________________ *the appointment this afternoon.*

4 Wir **haben** den Stadtplan **vergessen**.
We've ____________________ *the map.*

5 Wir haben den Stadtplan im Auto **vergessen**.
We've ____________________ *the map in the car.*

wandern – *wander*

➔ • wandern (gemächlich/ziellos streifen, bummeln) = *wander*
• wandern (eine Wanderung machen) = *hike, go hiking*

1 Sollen wir Samstag **wandern** gehen?
Shall we go ____________________ *on Saturday?*

2 Wir haben noch etwas Zeit. Wir können ein bisschen durch die Altstadt **wandern**.
We've still got some time left. We can ____________________ *a bit through the old town.*

3 Wie weit seid ihr heute **gewandert**? – 25 Kilometer.
How far did you ____________________ *today? – 25 kilometres.*

warm – ***warm***

> → • warm (generell) = *warm*
> • warm (zu warm, unangenehm warm) = *hot*
> • warm (in Bezug auf Wasser, Essen) = *hot*

1 Fahr lieber im Frühjahr. Im Sommer ist es oft zu **warm**.
I should go in the spring. In the summer it's often too ________________.

2 Es war ein schöner **warmer** Tag.
It was a nice ________________ *day.*

3 Ich hole dir eine **Wärm**flasche.
I'll get you a ________________*-water bottle.*

4 Einmal am Tag sollte man eine **warme** Mahlzeit zu sich nehmen.
You should have one ________________ *meal a day.*

5 Ein Zimmer mit **Warm**- und Kaltwasser.
A room with ________________ *and cold water.*

6 Mir ist zu **warm**. Ich ziehe die Jacke aus.
I'm ________________. *I'm going to take my jacket off.*

7 Ich mag es schön **warm** im Bett.
I like to have it nice and ________________ *in bed.*

vergessen 1forget 2left 3forget 4left ... behind / forgotten 5left **wandern** 1hiking 2wander 3hike **warm** 1hot 2warm 3hot 4hot 5hot 6hot 7warm

Übersetzen Sie die deutschen Wörter in Klammern ins Englische.

1 The car is old, but the (*Motor*) is still OK.

____

2 Can you (*bringen*) me to the station?

____

3 Restaurants with a small (*Karte*) are often very good.

____

4 Shall we go (*wandern*) on Sunday?

____

5 I'll try and (*leihen*) some chairs from my neighbours.

____

6 She developed the design (*allein*).

____

7 Shall we (*grillen*) this evening. The weather's so nice.

____

8 I've never eaten such a (*scharf*) curry.

____

9 We think it's a good idea. What do you (*meinen*), John?

____

10 Would anyone like a (*gekochtes*) egg?

____

11 In the test I had to decide if statements were true or (*falsch*).

____

12 My phone number is six (*Null*) three five seven.

____

13 What (*Programm*) do you watch most? – RTL.

____

14 We'll have a coffee (*Pause*) for 15 minutes.

____

15 I'll (*kochen*) some tea.

____

16 We had an increase of seven point (*Null*) three per cent.

____

17 I'm sorry. Dr Styles is (*außer Haus*).

____

18 If you wash the (*Salat*), I'll make the (*Soße*) for it.

____

19 Where is the (*nächste*) supermarket?

____

20 She has very little time at the moment. She (*lernt*) for her exam.

____

21 The address (*kommt*) in the top right-hand corner.

____

22 It's very cold here, eight degrees below (*Null*).

____

23 The (*Maschine*) is full, but I can put you on the waiting list.

____

24 The last bus has gone. How are we going to (*kommen*) home?

____

25 Have you heard the (*neuesten*) news?

____

[1]engine [2]take [3]menu [4]hiking [5]borrow [6]on her own / by herself [7]have a barbecue [8]hot / spicy [9]think [10]boiled [11]false [12]oh / zero [13]channel [14]break [15]make [16]nought / zero [17]out of the office / not in (the building) [18]lettuce, dressing [19]nearest [20]is studying [21]goes [22]zero [23]plane [24]get [25]latest

1.2 Wer die Wahl hat, hat die Qual

Ein Wort im Deutschen – mehrere Wörter im Englischen

Wählen Sie jeweils den richtigen Ausdruck aus und setzen Sie ihn ggf. in die richtige Form.

Arbeit

→
- Arbeit (allgemein oder Arbeitsort) = *work* [kann nicht mit *a/an* oder im Plural stehen!]
- Arbeit (einzelne, bestimmte Arbeit) = *job*
- Arbeit (Testarbeit in der Schule usw.) = *test*

work *job* *test*

1 Matthias schreibt morgen wieder eine Englisch**arbeit**.
Matthew is doing another English ________________ *tomorrow.*

2 Wie kommen Sie eigentlich zur **Arbeit**? – Mit dem Rad.
How do you come to ________________ *? – By bike.*

3 Tom sucht wieder eine Ferien**arbeit**. In den Weihnachtsferien ist es leicht, eine **Arbeit** zu finden.
Tom is looking for holiday ________________ *again. In the Christmas holidays it's easy to find a* ________________ .

4 Der Computer hat viele **Arbeiten** leichter gemacht.
The computer has made a lot of ________________ *much easier.*

aussteigen, einsteigen

→
- einsteigen (Auto, Taxi, kleines Boot) = *get in(to)*
- aussteigen (Auto, Taxi, kleines Boot) = *get out of*
- ein- / aufsteigen (Fahr- / Motorrad, Bus, Zug, Flugzeug, Schiff) = *get on(to)*
- ab-/aussteigen (Fahr- / Motorrad, Bus, Zug, Flugzeug, Schiff) = *get off*

get in *get on* *get out of* *get off*

1 In London bezahlt man, nachdem man aus dem Taxi **ausgestiegen ist.**
In London you pay after you ________________ the taxi.

2 Das kleine Boot hat arg gewackelt, als wir **einstiegen**.
The little boat was ever so wobbly when we ________________ .

3 Sie **stieg** auf ihr Motorrad **auf** und brauste davon.
She ________________ her motorbike and roared off.

4 Wo muss ich **aussteigen**? – An der nächsten Haltestelle.
Where do I have to ________________? – At the next stop.

(be)merken, (sich) merken

➔ • (be)merken (sich geistig bewusst werden) = *realize*
• (be)merken (mit den Sinnen wahrnehmen) = *notice*
• sich merken (zur Kenntnis nehmen und später daran denken) = *note/remember*

note notice realize

1 Er stand schon fünf Minuten im Dunkeln da, bevor ich ihn **bemerkte**.
He had been standing there in the dark for five minutes before I ________________ him.

2 Ich **merkte** plötzlich, dass ich die Adresse nicht dabei hatte.
I suddenly ________________ that I didn't have the address with me.

3 Ich **merkte**, dass er etwas in der linken Hand hielt.
I ________________ that he was holding something in his left hand.

4 **Merken Sie sich** bitte, dass Sie einen Pass brauchen werden.
Please ________________ that you will need a passport.

Arbeit 1test 2 work 3work [sonst: <u>a</u> *holiday job*], job 4work/jobs
aussteigen 1have got / get out of 2got in 3got on 4get off
bemerken 1noticed 2realized 4noticed 4note

bequem

> ➔ • bequem (körperliches Wohlbefinden vermittelnd) = *comfortable*
> • bequem (ohne Anstrengungen/Unannehmlichkeiten) = *easy*
> • bequem (faul) = *lazy*

comfortable *easy* *lazy*

1 Mein Kollege ist ein solch **bequemer** Mensch. Er tut fast nichts.
My colleague is such a ________________ person. He does hardly anything.

2 Dieser Pullover ist richtig **bequem**, ich liebe ihn.
This pullover is really ________________, I love it.

3 Die **bequemste** Lösung wäre, die Wohnung unterzuvermieten.
The ________________ solution would be to sub-let the flat.

bestellen

> ➔ • bestellen (Ware) = *order*
> • bestellen (Plätze, Tisch, Zimmer) = *book, reserve*
> • bestellen (Karten, Taxi) = [meist] *book*

book *order* *reserve*

1 Wer **bestellt** den Tisch für heute Abend?
Who's going to ________________ the table for this evening?

2 Das Taxi ist **bestellt**.
The taxi is ________________ .

3 **Bestell** mir bitte noch ein Bier.
________________ *me another beer, would you?*

4 Ich habe die Karten vor Monaten **bestellt**.
I ________________ the tickets months ago.

5 Ich **bestelle** normalerweise 250 Stück jeden Freitag.
I normally ________________ 250 every Friday.

besuchen

→	• besuchen (Menschen/Orte als Gast, Tourist usw. besuchen) = *visit* • besuchen (als Teilnehmer/in Einrichtungen wie Schule, Unterricht, Kirche besuchen) = *attend* (weniger förmlich auch: *go to*) • besuchen (kulturelle Veranstaltungen) = *go to*

attend *go to* *visit*

1 Mein Sohn **besuchte** eine Highschool in Texas.
My son _______________ a high school in Texas.

2 Am Wochenende **besuchen** wir Tante Agatha.
At the weekend we're _______________ing Aunt Agatha.

3 Wie viele **besuchen** noch regelmäßig den Gottesdienst?
How many still _______________ church regularly?

4 Gestern Abend **haben** wir ein Konzert **besucht**.
Yesterday evening we _______________ a concert.

5 Du musst unbedingt das Gruselkabinett **besuchen**.
You really must _______________ the chamber of horrors.

bequem [1]lazy [2]comfortable [3]easiest **bestellen** [1]book/reserve [2]booked [3]Order [4]booked [5]order **besuchen** [1]attended/went to [2]visit [3]attend/go to [4]went to [5]visit

(be)zahlen

→ • (be)zahlen (Produkt, Dienstleistung) = *pay for*
• (be)zahlen (Person, Betrag, Rechnung usw.) = *pay*

pay *pay for*

1 Der Verlag hat seinen Ghostwriter **bezahlt**.
The publisher ________________ *his ghost writer.*

2 Der Hauswirt soll die Reparatur **bezahlen**.
The landlord should ________________ *the repair.*

3 Hast du schon die Rechnung **bezahlt**?
Have you ________________ *the bill yet?*

4 Wer hat die Karten **bezahlt**?
Who ________________ *the tickets?*

5 Ich habe über $ 2000 **bezahlt**.
I ________________ *over $ 2000.*

bis

→ • bis (solange bis, die ganze Zeit bis [Frage: wie lange?]) = *until, till*
• bis (spätestens bis, nicht später als [Frage: wann? zu welchem Zeitpunkt?]) = *by*
• von … bis = *from … to*

by *till* *to*

1 Ich rufe dich spätestens **bis** sechs an.
I'll phone ________________ *six at the latest.*

2 Ich werde **bis** sechs warten, dann gehe ich heim.
I'll wait ________________ *six, then I'll go home.*

3 Er war von Kopf **bis** Fuß mit Schlamm bedeckt.
He was covered in mud from head ________________ *foot.*

4 Sie bekommen die Ware **bis** Freitag.
You'll get the goods ________________ Friday.

5 Er schlief **bis** zwölf.
He slept ________________ twelve.

bitte

→
- bitte (in Bitten, Aufforderungen, Fragen) = *please*
- bitte (bitte schön = Reaktion auf Dank) = *not at all, that's OK, it's a pleasure, that's all right, you're welcome, don't mention it*
- bitte (Reaktion auf Entschuldigung) = *it's/that's all right, never mind*
- bitte (Zustimmung zu Bitte) = *certainly; (yes,) of course; (yes,) please do*
- bitte? (wie bitte?) = *sorry? excuse me?*
- bitte (schön) (beim Überreichen) = *here you are*

please   not at all   it's all right   certainly   sorry?   here you are

1 Habe ich mich dazwischengedrängelt? Entschuldigung. – **Bitte**. Ich habe Zeit.
Have I barged in? Sorry. – ________________ . I have time.

2 Kannst du Sonia **bitte** anrufen?
Can you ring Sonia up, ________________?

3 Das war sehr freundlich von Ihnen. Vielen Dank. – **Bitte**.
That was very kind of you. Thank you. – ________________ .

4 Darf ich das Fenster aufmachen? – **Bitte**.
May I open the window? – ________________ .

5 **Wie bitte**? Das habe ich leider nicht verstanden.
________________? I'm afraid I didn't understand.

6 Eine heiße Schokolade, **bitte schön**. Vorsicht, sie ist sehr heiß.
One hot chocolate, ________________ . Careful, it's very hot.

bezahlen [1]paid [2]pay for [3]paid [4]paid for [5]paid **bis** [1]by [2]till [3]to [4]by [5]till
bitte [1]It's all right [2]please [3]Not at all [4]Certainly [5]Sorry? [6]here you are

bleiben

→
- bleiben (im gleichen Zustand bleiben) = *stay, keep;* (förmlicher auch:) *remain*
- bleiben (am gleichen Ort bleiben) = *stay;* (förmlicher auch:) *remain*
- bleiben (als Gast wohnen, übernachten) = *stay*
- bleiben (da-, weg-, fern-, auf-, aus-, draußen bleiben) = *stay*
- übrigbleiben = *remain,* (bei Sachen auch:) *be left (over)*

be left   *keep*   *remain*   *stay*

1 Tony **blieb** zu Hause.
Tony ________________ at home.

2 Wie lange **bleibt** deine Schwiegermutter?
How long is your mother-in-law going to ________________?

3 Tut mir Leid, aber ich kann nicht länger **dableiben**.
Sorry, I can't ________________ any longer.

4 Von dem alten Schloss ist wenig **geblieben**.
Little ________________ of the old castle.

5 Die Zuschauer **blieben** ganz still während der Sexszene.
The audience ________________ quite still during the sex scene.

6 **Bleib** draußen!
________________ out!

7 Sie **blieben** bis 4 Uhr auf.
They ________________ up till 4 in the morning.

Boden

→
- Boden (draußen) = *ground*
- Boden (Fußboden drinnen) = *floor*
- Boden (Nährboden, Erdreich) = *soil*
- Meeresboden = *seabed*

bed floor ground soil

1 Der **Boden** hier ist sehr fruchtbar.
The ________________ here is very fertile.

2 Sie lagen auf dem **Boden** im Wohnzimmer.
They were lying on the ________________ of the livingroom.

3 Sie legten sich auf den nassen **Boden**, zwischen den Blumen.
They lay down on the wet ________________, among the flowers.

4 Das Wrack wurde auf dem Meeres**boden** entdeckt.
The wreck was discovered on the sea________________ .

braten

→ • braten (in der Pfanne/im Topf oben auf dem Herd) = *fry*
• braten (im Backofen) = *roast*
• braten (auf dem Rost über/unter einem Grill) = *grill*

fry grill roast

1 Weihnachten? Er will wie jedes Jahr eine verdammte Gans **braten**.
Christmas? He wants to ________________ a blessed goose, like he does every year.

2 Zuerst die Zwiebeln und Kartoffeln in der Pfanne knusprig braun **braten**.
First ________________ the onions and potatoes in the frying pan till they're crisp and brown.

3 Nichts ist schöner, meint er, als ein dickes Steak auf dem Rost zu **braten**.
He thinks there's nothing nicer than to ________________ a big fat steak.

bleiben 1stayed/remained 2stay 3stay 4remains/is left 5stayed/kept/remained 6Stay 7stayed **Boden** 1soil 2floor 3ground 4bed **braten** 1roast 2fry 3grill

brauchen

→	• brauchen (etwas/jemanden benötigen) = *need* • brauchen (Zeit) = *take* • nicht brauchen (etwas zu tun) = *needn't/don't need to/don't have to (do something)*

need *needn't* *take*

1 Der Zug **braucht** zwei Stunden für die gleiche Strecke.
The train ________________ *two hours for the same distance.*

2 Du **brauchst** nicht zu kommen, wenn du nicht magst.
You ________________ *n't come if you don't want to.*

3 Wir **brauchen** sechs Freiwillige.
We ________________ *six volunteers.*

Daten

→	• Daten (Kalenderdaten) = *dates* • Daten (Informationen, Computerdaten) = *data*

data *dates*

1 Für das Treffen gibt es mehrere **Daten** zur Auswahl.
For the meeting there are several ________________ *to choose from.*

2 Nach dem Virus habe ich alle **Daten** auf der Festplatte verloren.
After the virus I lost all the ________________ *on my hard disk.*

dauern

→ • dauern (in Anspruch nehmen) = *take*
• dauern (andauern) = *last*

last *take*

1 Wie lange wird die Fahrt **dauern**?
How long will the journey ________________?

2 Das Konzert **dauerte** über zweieinhalb Stunden.
The concert ________________ over two and a half hours.

3 Das Packen **dauert** immer länger als das Auspacken.
The packing always ________________ longer than the unpacking.

eng

→ • eng (schmal) = *narrow*
• eng (eng anliegend, stramm) = *tight*

narrow *tight*

1 Diese Hose ist furchtbar **eng**.
These trousers are terribly ________________ .

2 Sie trägt gern ganz **enge** Röcke.
She likes wearing very ________________ skirts.

3 Die Straße war sehr **eng**.
The road was very ________________ .

brauchen [1]takes [2]need [3]need **Daten** [1]dates [2]data **dauern** [1]take [2]lasted [3]takes **eng** [1]tight [2]tight [3]narrow

Entschuldigung, entschuldigen Sie

> ➔ • Entschuldigung/entschuldigen Sie (bevor man etwas tut) = *excuse me*
> • Entschuldigung/entschuldigen Sie (nachdem man etwas getan hat) = *sorry*
> • Entschuldigung? (wie bitte?) = *sorry?/excuse me?*

excuse me *sorry*

1 War das Ihr Fuß? Oh, **Entschuldigung**.
Was that your foot? Oh, ________________ .

2 **Entschuldigung**? Könnten Sie das wiederholen?
________________? Could you repeat that?

3 **Entschuldigung**. Darf ich vorbei?
________________ . Can I come past?

erinnern

> ➔ • sich erinnern = *remember*
> • jemanden erinnern = *remind somebody*

remember *remind*

1 Ich **erinnere mich** an den schönen Wein, den wir dort getrunken haben.
I ________________ the lovely wine we drank there.

2 Wir haben uns mal bei Rita getroffen? **Erinnern Sie sich**?
We met once at Rita's. Do you ________________?

3 **Erinnere mich** bitte daran, Angela anzurufen.
Please ________________ to phone Angela.

Erinnerung

➔ • Erinnerung (Bild im Gedächtnis) = *memory*
• Erinnerung(sstück) = *souvenir*
• Erinnerung (Gedächtnisstütze) = *reminder*

memory *reminder* *souvenir*

1 Dieser Fußball ist ein **Erinnerungsstück** aus meiner Zeit in Texas.
This football is a ________________ *from my time in Texas.*

2 Welche **Erinnerungen** hast du an deine Schulzeit?
What ________________ *do you have of your schooldays?*

3 Ich lass' ihr einen Zettel, als **Erinnerung**.
I'll leave her a note as a ________________ .

erkennen

➔ • erkennen (mit den Sinnen wiedererkennen) = *recognize*
• erkennen (geistig entdecken) = *realize*
• den Unterschied erkennen = *tell the difference*

realize *recognize* *tell*

1 Ich **erkannte**, dass es sinnlos war, Damian um Hilfe zu bitten.
I ________________ *that it was pointless asking Damian for help.*

2 Kannst du den Unterschied **erkennen**? Welche ist die Designeruhr?
Can you ________________ *the difference? Which is the designer watch?*

3 Ich habe dich mit dem Bart nicht **erkannt**.
I didn't ________________ *you with the beard.*

Entschuldigung [1]sorry [2]Sorry? / Excuse me? [3]Excuse me
erinnern [1]remember [2]remember [3]remind me **Erinnerung** [1]souvenir [2]memories [3]reminder **erkennen** [1]realized [2]tell [3]recognize

fahren

→ • fahren (von A nach B kommen, ganz allgemein) = *go*
• fahren (Auto fahren, am Steuer sitzen, jemanden im Auto fahren) = *drive*
• fahren (Fahrrad, Motorrad) = *ride*
• fahren (als Fahrgast im Bus, Auto, Taxi) = *ride*
• fahren (+ Geschwindigkeitsangabe) = *travel*

drive go ride travel

1 Ich **fahre** in die Stadt.
I'm ________________ing to town.

2 Wo hast du **Autofahren** gelernt?
Where did you learn to ________________?

3 Mit 93 Jahren **fährt** er immer noch Motorrad.
He still ________________ a motorbike at 93.

4 Sie **fuhr** mit dem Bus nach Hause.
She ________________ home on the bus.

5 Ich **fahre** dich heim.
I'll ________________ you home.

6 Sie **fährt** nie in Urlaub.
She never ________________ on holiday.

7 Wer **fuhr** zum Zeitpunkt des Unglücks?
Who was ________________ing at the time of the accident?

8 Wir **fuhren** mit über 300 km/h.
We were ________________ing at over 300 kmh.

Farbe

> ➔ • Farbe (Rot, Grün, Blau usw.) = *colour*
> • Farbe (Mittel zum Anstreichen) = *paint*

colour *paint*

1 Die **Farbe** ist noch nicht trocken. Bitte nicht anfassen.
The ________________ is not dry. Please don't touch.

2 Wie viele Dosen **Farbe** soll ich kaufen?
How many cans of ________________ should I buy?

3 Welche **Farbe** hat das Auto?
What ________________ is the car?

fertig

> ➔ • fertig (bereit) = *ready*
> • fertig (erledigt, abgeschlossen) = *finished*

finished *ready*

1 Ich mache mich gerade **fertig**.
I'll just get ________________.

2 Die Arbeit ist **fertig**.
The work is ________________ .

3 Ich **bin** mit dem Abwasch **fertig**.
I ________________ the washing-up.

4 Wann ist das Mittagessen **fertig**?
When will lunch be ________________?

fahren [1]go [2]drive [3]rides [4]rode [5]drive [6]goes [7]driving [8]travelling
Farbe [1]paint [2]paint [3]colour **fertig** [1]ready [2]finished [3]have finished [4]ready

Frau, Mann

→
- Frau / Mann (weiblicher / männlicher Mensch) = *woman / man*
- Frau / Mann (Ehefrau / -mann) = *wife / husband*

husband man wife woman

1 Tinas **Mann** kocht sehr gut.
Tina's ________________ is a very good cook.

2 In diesem Kurs sind überwiegend **Frauen**.
There are mainly ________________ in this course.

3 **Männer** sind im Internet noch in der Mehrzahl.
________________ are still in the majority on the Internet.

4 Er hat **Frau** und Kinder überredet mitzufahren.
He persuaded his ________________ and children to go with him.

früher(e/er/es)

→
- früher (eher) = *earlier*
- früher einmal = *once*
- früher habe/bin ich (immer)... = *I used to ...*
- frühere(r/s) (vorhergehende/er/es) = *previous*
- frühere(r/s) (ehemalige/er/es) = *former*

earlier former once previous used to

1 Jimmy Carter ist ein **früherer** Präsident der USA.
Jimmy Carter is a ________________ president of the USA.

2 Warum bist du nicht **früher** gekommen?
Why didn't you come ________________?

3 **Früher** bin ich immer mit dem Zug zur Arbeit gefahren.
I ________________ travel to work by train.

4 **Früher** hatten wir einen Hund.
We ________________ have a dog.

5 **Früher einmal** hat er mich in sein Wochenendhäuschen eingeladen.
He ________________ invited me to his country cottage.

6 In unserer **früheren** Wohnung hatten wir keinen Balkon.
In our ________________ flat we didn't have a balcony.

gehen

➔
- gehen (allgemein) = *go*
- gehen (zu Fuß gehen im Gegensatz zu fahren) = *walk*
- gehen (verkehren) = *run, go*
- gehen (funktionieren) = *work*

go run walk work

1 Der letzte Bus war weg, also mussten wir **gehen**.
The last bus had gone, so we had to ________________ .

2 Tony ist schwimmen **gegangen**.
Tony's ________________ swimming.

3 Die Heizung **geht** nicht.
The heating isn't ________________ing.

4 Wo sind Sie zur Schule **gegangen**?
Where did you ________________ to school?

5 Es ist zu weit zu **gehen**.
It's too far to ________________.

6 Ich **gehe** mal gerade zu den Schmidts rüber.
I'm just ________________ing across to the Schmidts.

7 **Geht** der Zug auch sonntags?
Does the train ________________ on Sundays, too?

Frau, Mann ¹husband ²women ³Men ⁴wife **früher** ¹former ²earlier ³used to ⁴used to ⁵once ⁶previous **gehen** ¹walk ²gone ³work ⁴go ⁵walk ⁶going ⁷go / run

gesund

→	• gesund (robust, in guter körperlicher Verfassung) = *healthy, fit* • gesund (genesen) = *better* • gesund (gesundheitsfördernd) = *good for you*

better *fit* *good for you*

1 Ann war ziemlich krank, aber jetzt ist sie wieder **gesund**.
Ann was quite ill, but she's ________________ again now.

2 Um Pilotin zu werden, muss man **gesund** sein.
You have to be ________________ to become a pilot.

3 Obst ist **gesund**.
Fruit is ________________ .

4 Er ist mit 97 Jahren noch **gesund**.
He's still ________________ at 97.

5 Ich stimme Churchill zu: "No sports". Sport ist nicht **gesund**.
I agree with Churchill: "No sports". Sport isn't ________________ .

gewöhnlich

→	• gewöhnlich (üblich) = *usual* • gewöhnlich (alltäglich) = *ordinary* • gewöhnlich (ordinär) = *common*

common *ordinary* *usual*

1 Diese Großzügigkeit war sein **gewöhnlicher** Stil. Die Leute haben ihn geliebt.
This generosity was his ________________ style. People loved him.

2 Das Hotel war nicht Besonderes, ziemlich **gewöhnlich**.
The hotel wasn't anything special, pretty ________________ .

3 Die Braut trug eigentlich ein sehr **gewöhnliches** Kleid.
The bride was wearing a very ________________ *dress really.*

4 Der Mann hat überhaupt keine Manieren und ist ganz **gewöhnlich**.
The husband has no manners at all and is quite ________________ .

Grenze

→
- Grenze (Landesgrenze) = *border*
- Grenze (eines Grundstücks, Parks, Verwaltungsbezirks, US-Bundesstaats) = *boundary*
- Grenze (der maximal erreichbare/erreichte Punkt) = *frontier*
- Grenze (das zumutbare Ende) = *limit*

border *boundary* *frontier* *limit*

1 Ich habe die **Grenze** meiner Geduld erreicht.
I've reached the ________________ *of my patience.*

2 Wo sind heute die **Grenzen** der Naturwissenschaft? Weiß das noch jemand?
Where are the ________________ *of science today? Does anyone still know?*

3 Sie wohnen jenseits der Stadt**grenze**.
They live outside the town ________________ .

4 Wo liegt die Preis**grenze**?
What's the price ________________*?*

5 Wir wohnen in der Nähe der belgischen **Grenze**.
We live near the Belgian ________________ .

gesund [1]better [2]fit [3]good for you [4]fit [5]good for you **gewöhnlich** [1]usual [2]ordinary [3]ordinary [4]common **Grenze** [1]limit [2]frontiers [3]boundary [4]limit [5]border

groß

→
- groß (bei Sachen: physisch groß, ausgedehnt, umfangreich) = *big*
- groß (bei Menschen) = *tall* (hoch gewachsen), *big* (kräftig, stark; älter)
- groß (erfolgreich, umsatzstark) = *big*
- groß (beträchtlich) = *big, great* [vor Nomen, die keine Pluralform haben, ist nur *great* möglich]
- groß (großartig, berühmt, bedeutend) = *great*
- Großbuchstaben = *capital letters*

big great capital tall

1 Das ist mein **großer** Bruder.
This is my ________________ brother.

2 Man muss **große** Geduld haben.
You have to have ________________ patience.

3 Er hat **große** Schuhe, Größe 44.
He has ________________ shoes, size 44.

4 Irgendwie finde ich **große** Bahnhöfe faszinierend.
Somehow I find ________________ stations fascinating.

5 Auf meinem Urlaubszettel hatte er NEIN in **Groß**buchstaben geschrieben.
He had written NO in ________________ letters on my holiday form.

6 Das wäre natürlich ein **großer** Vorteil.
That would be a ________________ advantage, of course.

7 Sie hatte einen **großen** Fehler gemacht.
She had made a ________________ mistake.

8 Picasso war ein **großer** Künstler, einer der **größten**.
Picasso was a ________________ artist, one of the ________________ .

9 Wie **groß** sind Sie? – Ich bin 1,86 m **groß**.
How ________________ are you? – I'm 1 metre 86 ________________ .

10 Formel 1 ist ein **großes** Geschäft.
Formula 1 racing is ________________ business.

11 **Große** Hitze verträgt die Pflanze nicht.
The plant doesn't like ________________ heat.

12 Das macht keinen **großen** Unterschied.
That doesn't make a ________________ difference.

13 Basketballspieler müssen **groß** sein.
Basketball players have to be ________________ .

14 Kennedy hat eine **große** Rede gehalten.
Kennedy made a ________________ speech.

15 Gewichtheber sind meist **groß**.
Weightlifters are usually ________________ .

hören

→ • hören (akustisch wahrnehmen, verstehen) = *hear*
• hören (Radio, Musik) = *listen to*
• hören (zuhören, sich anhören, auf jemanden/etwas hören) = *listen (to)*

hear listen (to)

1 Was macht Anette? – Sie **hört** Musik.
What's Anette doing? – She's ________________ music.

2 Wenn man genau **hinhört**, merkt man den Akzent.
If you ________________ closely, you can notice the accent.

3 **Hörst** du etwas? – Ja, ein Ticken.
Can you ________________ anything? – Yes, a ticking sound.

groß 1big 2great 3big 4big 5capital 6big/great 7big/great 8great, greatest 9tall, tall 10big 11great 12big/great 13tall 14great 15big **hören** 1listening to 2listen 3hear

klein

> ➔ • klein (neutraler Ausdruck) = *small*
> • klein (gefühlsbetont, niedlichklein, unangenehm und klein) = *little*
> • klein (jünger) = *little*

Beachten Sie: *little* kann normalerweise nicht gesteigert werden (~~littler, littlest~~) und nicht hinter *be* stehen (~~The room is little.~~)

little *small*

1 Anna hat ein **kleines** Mädchen bekommen.
Anna has had a ________________ girl.

2 Die Wohnung ist relativ **klein**.
The flat is relatively ________________ .

3 Das ist mein **kleiner** Bruder.
That's my ________________ brother.

4 Sie hat ein hübsches **kleines** Zimmer.
She has a pretty ________________ room.

5 Wer ist **kleiner**, dein Bruder oder du?
Who is ________________, your brother or you?

6 Ihr Chef ist ein hässlicher **kleiner** Mann mit Glatze.
Her boss is an ugly ________________ man with a bald head.

7 Das Baby ist süß und sehr **klein**.
The baby is sweet and very ________________ .

8 Ein **Klein**wagen ist in der Stadt viel praktischer.
A ________________ car is much more practical in town.

9 Eine **kleine** Menge Zement genügt.
A ________________ amount of cement is enough.

krank

→ • krank (als Adjektiv, vor einem Nomen) = *sick* [Faustregel]
• krank (nach Verben wie *be*) = *ill* [Faustregel]

ill sick

1 Sie haben ein **krankes** Kind und mussten zu Hause bleiben.
They have a ________________ *child and had to stay at home.*

2 Tom ist **krank**. Hast du gehört?
Tom is ________________ *. Have you heard?*

3 Sie scheint ziemlich **krank** zu sein.
She seems to be pretty ________________ .

lebend

→ • lebend (im Gegensatz zu tot) = *living*
• lebend (echt, leibhaftig) = *live*

live living

1 Er hat einen **lebenden** Skorpion in der Wohnung.
He's got a ________________ *scorpion in his flat.*

2 Atwood ist vielleicht die bekannteste **lebende** kanadische Autorin.
Atwood is perhaps the greatest ________________ *Canadian female author.*

klein [1]little [2]small [3]little [4]little [5]smaller [6]little [7]small [8]small [9]small
krank [1]sick [2]ill [3]ill **lebend** [1]live [2]living

Lehrer / in

→	• Lehrer / in (für Kopfarbeit) = *teacher* • Lehrer / in (für praktische Fertigkeiten) = *instructor*

instructor   *teacher*

1 Unsere Nachbarin ist Hochschul**lehrerin**.
Our neighbour is a university ________________ .

2 Um Fahr**lehrer** zu sein, muss man eine Engelsgeduld haben.
You have to have the patience of a saint to be a driving ________________ .

3 Ski**lehrer** ist kein besonders romantischer Beruf.
Being a skiing ________________ *is not a very romantic job.*

4 Der Schwimm**lehrer** kann mit den Kleinen wirklich ganz gut.
The swimming ________________ *is really very good with the little kids.*

leicht

→	• leicht (im Gegensatz zu schwierig) = *easy* • leicht (geringfügig) = *slight* • leicht (von geringem Gewicht) = light

easy   *light*   *slight*

1 Es ist eine **leichte** Verbesserung eingetreten.
There has been a ________________ *improvement.*

2 Es fiel mir **leicht**, „nein" zu sagen.
I found it ________________ *to say "no".*

3 Der Koffer ist **leicht**, er ist fast leer.
The suitcase is ________________, *it's almost empty.*

4 Der Test war **leicht**.
The test was ________________ .

machen

→ • machen (herstellen, erzeugen, schaffen, basteln, bereitstellen) = *make* • machen (erledigen, verrichten, sich beschäftigen mit) = *do* • machen (in festen Wendungen) = *have, take, go* usw.

do go have make take

1 Ich **mache** jeden Morgen das Frühstück und den Kaffee.
I ________________ the breakfast and the coffee every morning.

2 Onkel Bernd **macht** ein Schläfchen nach dem Mittagessen.
Uncle Bernard ________________ a little sleep after lunch.

3 Sue **macht** Überstunden.
Sue is ________________ing overtime.

4 Wir haben einen guten Eindruck **gemacht**.
We ________________ a good impression.

5 **Macht** das einen großen Unterschied?
Does that ________________ a big difference?

6 Was **machst** du da unten auf dem Boden? – Ich **mache** meine Übungen.
What are you ________________ing down there on the floor? – I'm ________________ing my exercises.

7 Im Urlaub hat er 450 Fotos **gemacht**.
On holiday he ________________ 450 photos.

8 Wir **machen** gute Fortschritte.
We're ________________ing good progress.

9 Wenn es nicht regnet, **machen** wir ein Picknick.
If it doesn't rain, we'll ________________ a picnic.

Lehrer/in [1]teacher [2]instructor [3]instructor [4]instructor **leicht** [1]slight [2]easy [3]light [4]easy **machen** [1]make [2]has [3]do [4](have) made [5] make [6]do, do [7]took [8]making [9]have

10 Ich liebe es, Pläne zu **machen**.
I love ________________ing plans.

11 **Mach** Platz da.
Come on, ________________ room.

12 Wir sollten einen Anfang **machen**.
We should ________________ a start.

13 Warum **macht** die Regierung nichts?
Why doesn't the government ________________ something?

14 Wir **machen** Urlaub im Juni.
We're ________________ing on holiday in June.

15 Wann **machst** du die Prüfung?
When are you ________________ing the exam?

16 Wollen wir einen kleinen Spaziergang **machen**?
Shall we ________________ a little walk?

17 Wer **macht** bei euch den Abwasch?
Who ________________ the washing-up in your family?

18 Die Firma hat letztes Jahr Verlust **gemacht**.
Last year the firm ________________ a loss.

19 Ich habe einen großen Fehler **gemacht**.
I've ________________ a big mistake.

20 Ich **mache** (= putze) gleich die Schlafzimmer.
I'll ________________ the bedrooms in a minute.

21 Wir **machen** gute Geschäfte mit dieser Firma.
We ________________ good business with that firm.

22 Ich **mache** Ihnen ein Angebot/einen Vorschlag.
I'll ________________ you an offer/a suggestion.

23 Wer **macht** die Werbung für euch?
Who ________________ the advertising for you?

24 Was **machen Sie beruflich**?
What do you ________________ for a living?

25 **Machen** Sie das Beste daraus.
________________ *the best of it.*

26 Was hat dieses Geräusch **gemacht**?
What ________________ that noise?

27 Wann **machen** wir eine Pause?
When are we ________________ a break?

passen

> ➔ • passen (von der Größe, den Dimensionen her) = *fit*
> • passen (gut stehen) = *suit*
> • passen (zu etwas anderem, vom Stil / von der Farbe her) = *match*

fit match suit

1 Der Pullover **passt** gut zum Rock.
The pullover ________________ the skirt nicely.

2 Die Hose **passt** mir nicht mehr. Sie ist zu eng.
The trousers don't ________________ me any more. They're too tight.

3 **Passt** dieser Schlüssel?
Does this key ________________?

4 Der Pullover und der Rock **passen** gut zusammen.
The pullover and the skirt ________________ nicely.

5 Viel Make-up **passt** nicht zu ihr.
A lot of make-up doesn't ________________ her.

[10]making [11]make [12]make [13]do [14]going [15] taking/doing [16]have/take [17]does [18]made [19]made [20]do [21]do [22]make [23]does [24]do [25]Make [26]made [27]having/taking **passen** [1]matches [2]fit [3]fit [4]match [5]suit

Platz

> ➔ • Platz (Ort, Stelle; Studien-/Ausbildungsplatz) = *place*
> • Platz (ausreichend Raum) = *room, space*
> • Platz (Sitzplatz) = *seat*
> • Platz (in einer Stadt) = *square*
> • Platz (Sport) = *sports ground/playing field, court* (Tennis, Squash), *pitch* (Fußball), *course* (Golf)

course   court   place   seat   space   sports ground   square

1 Der **Sportplatz** ist schwer zu finden.
The ________________ *is difficult to find.*

2 Das ist ein schöner **Platz** für die Vase.
That's a nice ________________ *for the vase.*

3 Ich brauche einen **Platz**, wo ich meine Tasche abstellen kann.
I need a ________________ *where I can leave my bag.*

4 Sie wollen hier einen Golf**platz** anlegen.
They want to make a golf ________________ *here.*

5 Hast du noch **Platz** für diese Bücher in deinem Koffer?
Have you still got ________________ *for these books in your suitcase?*

6 Ist dieser **Platz** noch frei?
Is this ________________ *taken?*

7 Das Rathaus liegt an einem großen **Platz**.
The town hall is on a big ________________ .

8 Wir treffen uns auf dem Tennis**platz**.
We'll meet on the tennis ________________ .

9 Alle **Plätze** im Kurs waren weg.
All the ________________*s on the course were taken.*

10 Nehmen Sie **Platz**.
Have a ________________ .

Reise

→
- Reise (Reise generell, meist Vergnügungsreise einschl. Aufenthalt am Zielort) = *trip*
- Reise (längere Fahrt [ohne Aufenthalt am Zielort]) = *journey*
- das Reisen = *travel*
- Reisen (ausgedehnte Reise/n über längere Zeit) = *travels*
- Reise (Seereise) = *voyage*
- Rundreise = *tour*

journey tour travel travels trip voyage

1 Auf seinen **Reisen** begegnete Marco Polo faszinierenden Menschen.
On his ________________ Marco Polo met some fascinating people.

2 **Reisen** soll den Horizont erweitern.
________________ is supposed to broaden horizons.

3 Wir machen eine Wochenend**reise** nach London.
We're going on a weekend ________________ to London.

4 Die **Reise** dauerte 12 Stunden.
The ________________ took 12 hours.

5 Wie war eure [Urlaubs-]**Reise** nach Mexiko?
How was your ________________ to Mexico?

6 Hobbies: Sport, **Reisen**, Rockmusik.
Hobbies: sport, ________________, rock music

7 Kolumbus' Schiff kehrte nach einer **Reise** von 8 Monaten zurück.
Columbus' ship returned after an eight-month ________________ .

8 Eine **Rundreise** durch Skandinavien im Winter? – Nein danke.
A ________________ of Scandinavia in winter? – No thanks.

Platz 1sports ground 2place 3place 4course 5space 6seat 7square 8court 9place 10seat **Reise** 1travels 2Travel 3trip 4journey 5trip 6travel 7voyage 8tour

ruhig

➔ • ruhig (leise, ohne Lärm; nicht hektisch; unauffällig) = *quiet* • ruhig (ohne/mit wenig [unnötige/r] Bewegung) = *calm, still* (Sitzen), *steady* (Hand)

calm *quiet* *steady* *still*

1 Man braucht beim Operieren eine ganz **ruhige** Hand.
You need a really ________________ hand when you're operating.

2 Das Meer war Gott sei Dank **ruhig**.
The sea was ________________, thank goodness.

3 Das ist eine ziemlich **ruhige** Straße.
This is a pretty ________________ street.

4 Meine Tante führt ein **ruhiges** Leben.
My aunt leads a ________________ life.

5 Er saß ganz **ruhig** da.
He sat there quite ________________ .

6 Ich mag dieses **ruhige** Herbstwetter.
I like this ________________ autumn weather.

7 Die Kinder sind sehr **ruhig**. Was ist los?
The children are very ________________ . What's the matter?

sagen

➔ • sagen (aussprechen) = *say* • jemandem [etwas] sagen (jemandem [etwas] mitteilen) = *tell somebody (something)*

Beachten Sie: *tell* kann nicht ohne Nennung der angesprochenen Person verwendet werden. Ausnahmen: *tell a story* (eine Geschichte erzählen), *tell the truth* (die Wahrheit sagen), *tell lies* (lügen)

say *tell*

1 Tom hat nur wenig **gesagt**.
Tom didn't ________________ *much.*

2 Er **sagte** mir, wie ich dort hinkomme.
He ________________ *me how to get there.*

3 **Sagt** sie die Wahrheit? Was meinst du?
Is she ________________*ing the truth? What do you think?*

4 Er **sagte**: „Ich weiß es nicht."
He ________________, *"I don't know."*

5 Fabian **sagte** mir die Adresse.
Fabian ________________ *me the address.*

6 Daniela hat den ganzen Abend kein einziges Wort **gesagt**.
Daniela didn't ________________ *a single word all evening.*

Schatten

> ➔ • Schatten (schattiger Platz, vor der Sonne geschützt) = *shade*
> • Schatten (Schattenumriss einer Person / Sache) = *shadow*

shade *shadow*

1 Versuch doch irgendwo im **Schatten** zu parken.
Try and park somewhere in the ________________ .

2 Ich sah den **Schatten** eines Mannes an der Mauer.
I saw the ________________ *of a man on the wall.*

3 Er verfolgt mich ständig, wie ein **Schatten**.
He's constantly following me around, like a ________________ .

ruhig 1steady 2calm 3quiet 4quiet 5still 6calm 7quiet **sagen** 1say 2told 3tell 4said 5told 6say **Schatten** 1shade 2shadow 3shadow

(sich) (an-/hin)schauen / sehen

→
- (hin)schauen (bewusstes, aufmerksames Richten der Augen auf etwas) = *look*
- (sich) etwas / jemanden anschauen = *look at*
- (sich) etwas / jemanden längere Zeit anschauen (verfolgen, beobachten) = *watch*

Beachten Sie: *watch* kann nur bei etwas Bewegtem / Beweglichem gebraucht werden.

look   *look at*   *watch*

1 Wir haben das Feuerwerk vom Balkon aus **angeschaut**.
We ________________ *the firework display from our balcony.*

2 Sie **sah** mich **an**, als käme ich vom Mars.
She ________________ *me as if I came from Mars.*

3 Sie küssen sich gerade. **Schau** jetzt nicht **hin**!
They're just kissing. Don't ________________ *now.*

4 **Sieh** dir dieses Bild hier **an**.
________________ *this picture here.*

5 Willst du dir das Fußballspiel **ansehen**?
Are you going to ________________ *the football match?*

6 **Schau**, ein Kaninchen!
________________, *a rabbit!*

7 Sie **sah** sich das Foto mehrere Minuten **an**.
She ________________ *the photo for several minutes.*

schlafen

→	• schlafen (in Bezug auf Schlafgewohnheiten, Schlafdauer, Schlafqualität, vorübergehende Schlafweise) = *sleep* • schlafen (im Zustand des Schlafens sein) = *be asleep*

be asleep *sleep*

1 Ich **schlafe** sieben Stunden.

I ________________ *seven hours.*

2 Wo ist Tim? – Er **schläft**.

Where's Tim? – He ________________ .

3 Ich habe **geschlafen**, als der Maler kam.

I ________________ *when the painter came.*

4 Wir **schliefen** bis halb drei, dann hat der Bergführer uns geweckt.

We ________________ *till 2.30 then the guide woke us.*

5 Die Kinder **schlafen**.

The children ________________ .

6 Haben Sie gut **geschlafen**?

Did you ________________ *well?*

7 Sie **schläft** sehr unruhig heute Abend.

She ________________ *very restlessly this evening.*

schauen [1]watched [2]looked at [3]look [4]Look at [5]watch [6]Look [7]looked at
schlafen [1]sleep [2]is asleep [3]was asleep [4]slept [5]are asleep [6]sleep [7]is sleeping

schnell

→	• schnell (von der Bewegung / Bewegungsmöglichkeit her) = *fast* • schnell (nur kurze Zeit beanspruchend) = *quick*

fast *quick*

1 Werfen wir einen **schnellen** Blick in die alte Kirche.
Let's have a ________________ *look in the old church.*

2 Es war immer mein Traum, einen **schnellen** Wagen zu haben.
I've always dreamed of having a ________________ *car.*

3 Es ist eine **schnelle** Straße. Man kommt gut voran.
It's a ________________ *road. You can get on.*

4 Ich brauche eine **schnelle** Antwort: ja oder nein.
I need a ________________ *answer: yes or no.*

5 Er ist ein sehr **schneller** Läufer.
He's a very ________________ *runner.*

6 Wir nahmen eine **schnelle** Mahlzeit zu uns und waren schon wieder unterwegs.
We had a ________________ *meal and were off again.*

schwer

→	• schwer (von Gewicht) = *heavy* • schwer (schwierig) = *difficult, hard* • schwer (ernsthaft) = *serious* • schwer (in festen Wendungen): *bad, hard, stinking* usw.

bad(ly) *difficult* *hard* *heav(il)y* *serious(ly)* *stinking*

1 Sie hatte eine **schwere** Verletzung.
She had a ________________ *injury.*

2 Mann, ist der Koffer **schwer**.
Goodness, the suitcase is ________________ .

3 Mein Onkel ist sehr **schwer**hörig.
My uncle is very ________________ *of hearing.*

4 Die Prüfung war verdammt **schwer**.
The exam was bloody ________________ .

5 Ich musste **schwer** arbeiten.
I had to work ________________ .

6 Es war eine sehr **schwere** Entscheidung.
It was a very ________________ *decision.*

7 Das ist **schwer** zu verstehen / sich vorzustellen, ich weiß.
That's ________________ *to understand / imagine, I know.*

8 Ich hatte einen **schweren** Fehler gemacht.
I had made a ________________ *mistake.*

9 Ich war **schwer** enttäuscht.
I was ________________ *disappointed.*

10 Sie kann nicht singen. Sie hat eine **schwere** Erkältung.
She can't sing. She has a ________________ *cold.*

11 Um das Parlamentsgebäude tobten **schwere** Kämpfe.
There was ________________ *fighting round the parliament building.*

12 Seine Tante ist **schwer**reich.
His aunt is ________________ *rich.*

13 Der Boden hier oben ist furchtbar **schwer**.
The soil up here is very ________________ .

schnell [1]quick [2]fast [3]fast [4]quick [5]fast [6]quick **schwer** [1]serious [2]heavy [3]hard [4]difficult/hard [5]hard [6]difficult/hard [7]difficult/hard [8]serious [9]badly [10]bad [11]heavy [12]stinking [13]heavy

seit

➔	• seit (ab dem Zeitpunkt [Frage: seit wann?]) = *since* • seit (während, lang [Frage: wie lange?]) = *for*

for *since*

1 Ich habe sie **seit** letztem Jahr nicht mehr gesehen.
I haven't seen her ________________ last year.

2 Ich warte **seit** sechs Uhr darauf, dass er anruft.
I've been waiting for him to phone ________________ six o'clock.

3 Ich warte **seit** mehr als zwei Stunden.
I've been waiting ________________ more than two hours.

4 Wir haben uns **seit** einer Ewigkeit nicht mehr gesprochen.
We haven't spoken ________________ ages.

Spiel

➔	• Spiel (Zeitvertreib, nette Beschäftigung – generell) = *game* • Spiel (offizieller Wettkampf) = *match*

game *match*

1 „Monopoly“ ist ein weltbekanntes **Spiel**.
"Monopoly" is a world-famous ________________ .

2 Die Kinder erfinden immer neue **Spiele**.
The children are always thinking up new ________________ .

3 Heute Abend läuft ein Fußball**spiel** im Fernsehen.
There's a football ________________ on TV this evening.

4 Wir könnten mal heute Abend ein **Kartenspiel** machen.
We could have a ________________ of cards this evening.

stark

> ➔ • stark (kräftig) = *strong*
> • stark (schwer, heftig) = *heavy*

heavy *strong*

1 Der Regen war sehr **stark**.
The rain was very ________________ .

2 **Starke** Raucher sind besonders gefährdet.
________________ *smokers are especially at risk.*

3 Oben auf dem Berg war der Wind richtig **stark**.
Up on the top of the mountain the wind was really ________________ .

Straße

> ➔ • Straße (Verkehrsweg, -fläche; Straße außerhalb von Ortschaften) = *road*
> • Straße (innerorts mit Gebäuden, Teil einer Wohn- oder Geschäftsgegend) = *street*

road *street*

1 Er blieb mitten auf der **Straße** stehen.
He stopped in the middle of the ________________ .

2 Es gibt viele kleine **Straßen** um den Dom.
There are a lot of little ________________ *round the cathedral.*

3 Die **Straßen** in diesem Stadtteil sind sicher, auch nachts.
The ________________ *in this part of the town are safe, also at night.*

4 Ist das die **Straße** nach Detmold?
Is this the ________________ *to Detmold?*

seit [1]since [2]since [3]for **Spiel** [1]game [2]games [3]match [4]game **stark** [1]heavy [2]Heavy [3]strong **Straße** [1]road [2]streets [3]streets [4]road

tragen

→	• tragen (mitführen, befördern) = *carry* • tragen (im übertragenen Sinne) = *bear* • tragen (hochhalten) = *support* • tragen (am Körper anhaben) = *wear*

bear carry support wear

1 Du **trägst** die Verantwortung.
You ________________ the responsibility.

2 Sie **trug** einen Armreif aus purem Gold.
She was ________________ a bracelet made of pure gold.

3 **Tragen** Polizisten Schusswaffen in diesem Land?
Do police officers ________________ guns in this country?

4 An deiner Stelle würde ich keine Jeans zum Vorstellungsgespräch **tragen**.
If I were you, I wouldn't ________________ jeans to an interview.

5 Diese vier Balken **tragen** das ganze Obergeschoss.
These four beams ________________ the whole of the upper storey.

6 Wer wird die Kosten **tragen** müssen?
Who will have to ________________ the costs?

7 Das Wasser ist so salzhaltig, dass man davon **getragen** wird.
The water is so salty that it ________________ you.

8 Wer **trägt** mir den Koffer rein?
Who's going to ________________ my suitcase inside for me?

9 Endlich fangen unsere vielen Anstrengungen an Früchte zu **tragen**.
At last our efforts are beginning to ________________ fruit.

verstehen

> ➔ • verstehen (begreifen) = *understand*
> • verstehen (akustisch wahrnehmen) = *hear*

hear *understand*

1 Ich **verstehe** nicht, warum er nicht wartet.
I don't ________________ *why he doesn't wait.*

2 Es war so laut, ich konnte ihn nicht richtig **verstehen**.
It was so noisy, I couldn't ________________ *him properly.*

vor

> ➔ • vor (räumlich) = *in front of*
> • vor (zeitlich, Gegenteil von „nach") = *before,* (bei Uhrzeit:) *to*
> • vor (zeitlich, im Sinne von „her") = *ago*

ago *before* *in front of* *to*

1 Ich war **vor** Ihnen da!
I was here ________________ *you!*

2 Ein großer Mann saß genau **vor** mir.
A tall man sat right ________________ *me.*

3 Wir treffen uns um zehn **vor** sechs.
We'll meet at ten ________________ *six.*

4 Ich habe ihn zuletzt **vor drei Tagen** gesehen.
I last saw him ________________ .

5 Ich rufe **vor** dem Abendessen an.
I'll call ________________ *supper.*

tragen [1]bear [2]wearing [3]carry [4]wear [5]support [6]bear [7]supports [8]carry [9]bear **verstehen** [1]understand [2]hear **vor** [2]before [2]in front of [3]to [4]three days ago [5]before

während

→ • während (leitet Satz ein) = *while*
• während (steht vor einem Nomen) = *during*

during *while*

1 **Während** ich schlief, räumten sie die Wohnung aus.
________________ *I slept, they emptied the flat.*

2 **Während** des Vormittags gehen die meisten Anrufe ein.
Most calls come in ________________ *the morning.*

3 **Während** des Vorstellungsgeprächs fing er an zu zittern.
He started to tremble ________________ *the interview.*

4 Der Briefträger kam, **während** ich wartete.
The postman came ________________ *I was waiting.*

wohnen

→	• wohnen (zu Hause sein) = *live* • wohnen (vorübergehend als Gast untergebracht sein) = *stay*

live *stay*

1 Wir **wohnen** im Hotel Hyatt.
We're ________________ at the Hyatt Hotel.

2 Wie lange **wohnen** Sie hier schon? – Zehn Jahre.
How long have you been ________________ here now? – Ten years.

3 Wenn ich nach London fahre, **wohne** ich meist bei Freunden.
When I go to London, I usually ________________ with friends.

während [1]While [2]during [3]during [4]while **wohnen** [1]staying [2]living [3]stay

Übersetzen Sie die deutschen Wörter in Klammern ins Englische.

1 We were (*früher einmal*) invited to a party by a film star.

2 Are you (*fertig*) with the photocopier now? Can I use it?

3 Have you (*bestellt*) the table at the Indian restaurant yet?

4 Fruit and salad are (*gesund*). Come on, have some more.

5 I'll let you know (*bis*) Saturday if I can come or not.

6 Who is the children's swimming (*Lehrer*)?

7 It's a big repair. It will (*dauern*) some time.

8 When will you (*machen*) your exam?

9 I suddenly (*bemerkte*) that I didn't know her surname.

10 The pullover doesn't (*passen zum*) the trousers very well.

11 It's so cold in here. – Yes, the heating (*geht nicht*) today, I'm afraid.

12 These jeans are very (*eng*). I have to go on a diet.

13 Tony (*sagte*) me that he could help.

14 I had to sleep on the (*Boden*) in the livingroom.

____

15 This flat is (*kleiner*) than our old one.

____

16 Where do I have to (*aussteigen*)? – At the next stop.

____

17 Is this the (*Straße*) to Gainsville?

____

18 It all (*braucht*) time. Don't be in such a hurry.

____

19 Who's going to (*fahren*) home from the party, you or me?

____

20 Where do their children (*besuchen*) school?

____

21 We went on a great (*Reise*) to Canada last autumn.

____

22 (*Erinnere*) me to phone Don this evening.

____

23 Who is going to (*bezahlen*) the damage?

____

24 Many people in Africa are in (*großer*) need.

____

25 I (*erkannte*) that it was silly to wait any longer.

____

[1]once [2]finished [3]booked/reserved [4]good for you [5]by [6]instructor [7]take [8]do/take [9]realized [10]match [11]isn't working [12]tight [13]told [14]floor [15]smaller [16]get off [17]road [18]takes [19]drive [20]attend/go to [21]trip [22]Remind [23]pay for [24]great [25]realized

1.3 Achtung, falscher Freund!

Deutsch-englische Wortpaare, die gleich aussehen, aber Unterschiedliches bedeuten

Vervollständigen Sie das Lösungswort.

Aktion – *action*

> ➔ • *action* = Tat, Handlung, Handeln
> *I want to see* ***action****, not words!* = Ich will Taten sehen, nicht Worte!

1 Für den Herbst planen wir eine große Werbe**aktion**.
For the autumn we're planning a big advertising cam__________.

2 200 Polizisten waren an der Rettungs**aktion** beteiligt.
200 police officers took part in the rescue op__________.

aktuell – *actual(ly)*

> ➔ • *actual(ly)* = tatsächlich
> *We did* ***actually*** *see a leopard.* = Wir haben tatsächlich einen Leoparden gesehen.

1 Dieser Fahrplan ist nicht mehr **aktuell**. [= gültig]
This timetable is longer va__________.

2 Das Thema des Films ist sehr **aktuell**. [= wichtig, von momentanem Interesse]
The subject of the film is very to__________.

3 Die Nachrichten sind voll der **aktuellen** Ereignisse in Iran. [= gegenwärtig]
The news is full of the cu__________ events in Iran.

Allee – *alley*

→	• *alley* = Gasse / schmaler Weg *an **alley** by the side of the supermarket* = ein schmaler Weg neben dem Supermarkt

1 Die Straße zum Schloss war eine **Allee** mit wunderschönen Buchen.
The road to the castle was an av__________ of beautiful beech trees.

Ambulanz – *ambulance*

→	• *ambulance* = Krankenwagen *He was taken to hospital in an **ambulance**.* = Er wurde mit dem Krankenwagen ins Krankenhaus gebracht.

1 Die **Ambulanz** war voll und ich musste zwei Stunden warten.
The out-pa__________' department was full and I had to wait two hours.

annoncieren – *announce*

→	• *announce* = bekannt geben, ankündigen ***announce** one's resignation* = seinen Rücktritt bekannt geben

1 Wir haben **annonciert** und über 300 Bewerbungen erhalten.
We adv__________ed and received over 300 applications.

Aktion [1]campaign [2]operation **aktuell** [1]valid [2]topical [3]current
Allee [1]avenue **Ambulanz** [1]out-patients' **annoncieren** [1]advertised

bekommen – *become*

➔	• *become* = werden *Elizabeth* ***became*** *Queen in 1953.* = Elizabeth wurde Königin im Jahre 1953.

1 Wir **bekommen** viele Anfragen aus dem Ausland.
We __________ a lot of enquiries from abroad.

2 Astrid **hat** ein Baby **bekommen**, einen kleinen Jungen.
Astrid has __________ a baby, a little boy.

blamieren – *blame*

➔	• *blame* = die Schuld geben *The boss* ***blamed*** *me.* = Der Chef gab mir die Schuld.

1 In dem Interview hat er sich richtig blamiert.
In the interview he m__________ a real f__________l of himself.

blinken – *blink*

➔	• *blink* = blinzeln ***blink*** *when you come into the sunlight* = blinzeln, wenn man in die Sonne kommt

1 Der Fahrer hat links **geblinkt** und ist dann rechts abgebogen.
The driver indi__________ left, then turned off right.

Branche – *branch*

→	• *branch* = Zweigstelle *a **branch** of Lloyds Bank* = eine Zweigstelle der Lloyds Bank

1 Ich arbeite in der Werbe**branche**.
I'm in the advertising bus__________.

brav – *brave*

→	• *brave* = mutig, tapfer *a **brave** woman* = eine mutige Frau

1 Die Kinder waren den ganzen Abend **brav**.
The children were g__________ all evening.

Chef – *chief, chef*

→	• *chief* = „Häuptling"; *chef* = „Koch / Küchenchef" *an Apache **chief*** = ein Apachenhäuptling *The **chef** served the dessert himself.* = Der Koch servierte den Nachtisch selbst.

1 Wie ist dein neuer **Chef**?
What's your new b__________ like?

2 Das ist unserere neue **Chef**ingenieurin / **Chef**redakteurin / **Chef**designerin.
That's our new c__________ engineer/c__________ editor/ c__________ designer.

bekommen [1]get/have/receive [2]had **blamieren** [1]made a real fool of himself **blinken** [1]indicated **Branche** [1]business **brav** [1]good **Chef** [1]boss [2]chief (Ausnahme)

City – *city*

→	• *city* = Großstadt *the **city** of New York* = die Großstadt New York

1 Sie will ein neues Geschäft in der **City** eröffnen.
She wants to open a new shop in the town/city cen__________.

Direktion – *direction*

→	• *direction* = Richtung *Which **direction** is the sea?* = In welcher Richtung liegt das Meer?

1 Die **Direktion** hat das gestern beschlossen.
The man__________ decided yesterday.

engagiert – *engaged*

→	• *engaged* = verlobt *They've been **engaged** for 12 years.* = Sie sind seit 12 Jahren verlobt.

1 Sie ist in der Lokalpolitik stark **engagiert**.
She's heavily inv__________ in local politics.

eventuell – *eventually*

→	• *eventually* = schließlich, endlich *I got used to things **eventually**.* = Ich habe mich schließlich an die Situation gewöhnt.

1 Ich komme **eventuell** nicht, ich kann es noch nicht versprechen.
I m__________ not come, I can't promise yet.

Fabrik – *fabric*

→	• *fabric* = Stoff *What **fabric** is this made from?* = Aus welchem Stoff ist das?

1 Neue **Fabriken** entstanden auf der grünen Wiese.
New f__________ were built on green-field sites.

fatal – *fatal*

→	• *fatal* = tödlich; verhängnisvoll *a **fatal** accident, a **fatal** mistake* = ein tödlicher Unfall, ein verhängnisvoller Fehler

1 Der Rechtstreit war eine **fatale** Sache.
The lawsuit was an unfor__________ affair.

Flur – *floor*

→	• *floor* = Fußboden; Etage *sit on the **floor**, a flat on the 10th **floor*** = auf dem Fußboden sitzen, eine Wohnung in der 10. Etage

1 Der **Flur** war schmal und dunkel.
The h__________ was narrow and dark.

City 1centre **Direktion** 1management **engagiert** 1involved **eventuell** 1may **Fabrik** 1factories **fatal** 1unfortunate **Flur** 1hall

Formular – *formula*

→	• *formula* = Formel *a mathematical **formula*** = eine mathematische Formel

1 Ich musste drei **Formulare** ausfüllen.
I had to fill in three ________________s.

Fotograf – *photograph*

→	• *photograph* = Fotografie *a black-and-white **photograph*** = eine Schwarz-Weiß-Fotografie

1 Er arbeitet als **Fotograf** bei einer Werbeagentur.
He works as a ________________ for an advertising agency.

Gasthaus – *guesthouse*

→	• *guesthouse* = Pension *a **guesthouse** in a seaside town* = eine Pension in einer Stadt am Meer

1 Wir aßen zu Mittag in einem alten **Gasthaus** auf dem Land.
We had lunch in an old country i________________.

Gift – *gift*

→	• *gift* = Geschenk *a **gift** shop* = ein Geschenkeladen

1 ein tödliches **Gift**
a deadly poi________________

Gymnasium – *gymnasium*

→	• *gymnasium* = Turn-/Sporthalle *play badminton in the* ***gymnasium*** = Badminton in der Turnhalle spielen

1 In Großbritannien sind die **Gymnasien** fast alle abgeschafft.
In Britain nearly all the g________________ schools have been abolished.

Handy – *handy*

→	• *handy* [Adjektiv] = praktisch, griffbereit *It's* ***handy*** *to have a doctor as a neighbour.* = Es ist praktisch einen Arzt als Nachbarn zu haben.

1 Meine **Handy**nummer ist 0123-41018197.
My m________________ number is 0123-41018197.

Hausmeister – *housemaster*

→	• *housemaster* = Internatsleiter *the* ***housemaster*** *at a boarding school* = der Internatsleiter an einer Internatsschule

1 Der **Hausmeister** hat mir mit einem Doppelstecker ausgeholfen.
The care ________________ helped me out with an adapter.

Formular [1]forms **Fotograf** [1]photographer **Gasthaus** [1]inn **Gift** [1]poison **Gymnasium** [1]grammar **Handy** [1]mobile **Hausmeister** [1]caretaker

Hochschule – *high school*

➔	• *high school* = weiterführende Schule (in den USA) *leave **high school** and get a job* = von der Highschool abgehen und eine Arbeit aufnehmen

1 An welcher **Hochschule** haben Sie studiert?
Which u________________ did you study at?

irritieren – *irritate*

➔	• *irritate* = nerven *This tapping is beginning to **irritate** me.* = Dieses Klopfen beginnt mir auf die Nerven zu gehen.

1 Ich bin ganz **irritiert**. Ich weiß nicht mehr, wo ich anfangen soll.
I'm completely con________________. I don't know where to start.

Kaution – *caution*

➔	• *caution* = Vorsicht *We must proceed with **caution**.* = Wir müssen mit Vorsicht vorgehen.

1 zwei Monatsmieten **Kaution**
two months rent as a dep________________

2 Er wurde gegen **Kaution** freigelassen.
He was released on ba________________.

Keks – *cake*

➔	• *cake* = Kuchen *a piece of chocolate* ***cake*** = ein Stück Schokoladenkuchen

1 Bitte stellen Sie noch ein paar **Kekse** hin.
Please put out a few (BE:) b________________ /(AE:) c________________, too.

komfortabel – *comfortable*

➔	• *comfortable* = bequem *a nice* ***comfortable*** *chair* = ein schöner bequemer Sessel

1 Sie besitzen eine sehr **komfortable** Wohnung in einem bevorzugten Wohngebiet.
They own a very lux________________ flat in an exclusive area.

konsequent – *consequent*

➔	• *consequent* = daraus resultierend *Oil prices doubled and the* ***consequent*** *rise in inflation …* = Die Ölpreise haben sich verdoppelt und der daraus resultierende Inflationsanstieg …

1 Sie kämpfte **konsequent** für die Modernisierung.
She fought consi________________ for modernization.

Hochschule [1]university **irritieren** [1]confused **Kaution** [1]deposit [2]bail **Keks** [1]biscuits / cookies **komfortabel** [1]luxurious **konsequent** [1]consistently

kontrollieren – *control*

→ • *control* = kontrollieren (= unter Kontrolle haben/halten); steuern, regeln
Big firms ***control*** *the market.* = Große Firmen kontrollieren den Markt.
He can't ***control*** *his children.* = Er kann seine Kinder nicht unter Kontrolle halten.
This robot ***controls*** *the whole process.* = Dieser Roboter steuert das ganze Verfahren.

1 Unsere Fahrkarten sind kein einziges Mal **kontrolliert** worden.
Our tickets weren't c________________ed once.

Konzept – *concept*

→ • *concept* = Begriff
The Internet was a new ***concept*** *then.* = Das Internet war damals ein neuer Begriff.

1 Bis zum Jahresende soll das **Konzept** stehen.
The pl________________ is to be completed by the end of the year.

Kritik – *critic*

→ • *critic* = Kritiker/in, Rezensent/in
His son was his harshest ***critic***. = Sein Sohn war sein schärfster Kritiker.

1 Hast du die **Kritik** gelesen? In der gestrigen Ausgabe?
Have you read the rev________________? In yesterday's edition?

Lust – *lust*

➔	• *lust* = Begierde, Wollust *the victim of* ***lust*** = das Opfer der Begierde

1 Ich habe **Lust** am Wochenende wegzufahren.
I feel l_________________ going away for the weekend.

Mappe – *map*

➔	• *map* = (Land-)Karte, Plan *show me on the* ***map*** = zeig es mir auf der Karte

1 Ich brauche die **Mappe** mit den Rechnungen vom Juni.
I need the fo_________________er with the June bills.

Marke – *mark*

➔	• *mark* = (Zensur-)Note; Fleck *The teacher gave me a good* ***mark****.* = Die Lehrerin gab mir eine gute Note. *a* ***mark*** *on the table* = ein Fleck auf dem Tisch

1 Welche **Marke** kaufen Sie?
What br_________________ do you buy?

2 Man tauscht die **Marke** an der Theke ein.
You exchange your vou_________________ at the counter.

kontrollieren [1]checked **Konzept** [1]plan **Kritik** [1]review **Lust** [1]like
Mappe [1]folder **Marke** [1]brand [2]voucher

Meinung – *meaning*

→ • *meaning* = Bedeutung
*the **meaning** of a word* = die Bedeutung eines Wortes

1 Wie ist Ihre **Meinung**?
What's your o________________?

Mörder – *murder*

→ • *murder* = Mord
*the sixth **murder** this month* = der sechste Mord in diesem Monat

1 Die Polizei hat den vermutlichen **Mörder** geschnappt.
The police have caught the suspected m________________.

Note – *note*

→ • *note* = Notiz, Zettel
*make **notes*** = Notizen machen
*I'll write her a **note**.* = Ich schreibe ihr einen Zettel.

1 Welche **Note** hat der Englischlehrer gegeben?
What m________________ did the Engish teacher give?

Notiz – *notice*

→ • *notice* = Anschlag; Kündigungsfrist
*hang a **notice** on the wall* = einen Anschlag an der Wand anbringen
*six months **notice*** = sechs Monate Kündigungsfrist

1 Ich kann die eigenen **Notizen** nicht mehr lesen.
I can't read my own n________________ any more.

Oldtimer – *oldtimer*

→ • *oldtimer* = alter Knabe, alter Hase
*an **oldtimer** who has lived here for 50 years* = ein alter Knabe, der seit 50 Jahren hier lebt

1 Millionäre können es sich leisten, **Oldtimer** zu sammeln.
Millionaires can afford to collect vet________________ cars.

Paket – *packet*

→ • *packet* = Päckchen
*a **packet** of biscuits/butter/tea* = ein Päckchen Kekse/Butter/Tee

1 Zwei Tage vor dem Geburtstag kam ein Riesen**paket** an.
Two days before the birthday a huge par________________ arrived.

2 Welches Software**paket** benutzen Sie?
What software pack________________ do you use?

Personal – *personal*

→ • *personal* = persönlich
***personal** phone calls* = persönliche Telefongespräche

1 Das ist der **Personal**eingang.
This is the st________________ entrance.

Meinung [1]opinion **Mörder** [1]murderer **Note** [1]mark **Notiz** [1]notes
Oldtimer [1]veteran **Paket** [1]parcel [2]package **Personal** [1]staff

Phrase – *phrase*

→	• *phrase* = Ausdruck, Wendung *learn words in a* ***phrase*** = Wörter in einer Wendung lernen

1 Nichts als leere **Phrasen**!
Nothing but empty cli_________________és.

plump – *plump*

→	• *plump* = mollig *a* ***plump*** *lady in a white hat* = eine mollige Dame mit einem weißen Hut

1 Er machte ziemlich **plumpe** Erklärungsversuche.
He made pretty cl_________________ attempts to explain himself.

Promotion – *promotion*

→	• *promotion* = Beförderung ***promotion*** *after only six months* = Beförderung schon nach sechs Monaten

1 Wann wollen Sie Ihre **Promotion** abschließen?
When do you want to finish your doc_________________ ?

Prospekt – *prospect*

→	• *prospect* = Aussicht *the* ***prospects*** *of improvement* = die Aussichten auf eine Verbesserung

1 Ein Messestand ohne **Prospekte**?!
A stall at the fair without br_________________ ?!

Provision – *provision*

→	• *provision* = Bereitstellung *the* ***provision*** *of tents for the earthquake victims* = die Bereitstellung von Zelten für die Opfer des Erdbebens

1 Er verdient 7% **Provision** bei jedem Vertrag.
He earns 7% comm________________ on every contract.

Reklamation – *reclamation*

→	• *land reclamation* = Landgewinnung *the* ***reclamation*** *of land by building dikes* = Landgewinnung durch Eindeichung

1 Ich möchte mit dem Manager sprechen. Ich habe eine **Reklamation**.
I would like to speak to the manager. I have a c________________.

Rente – *rent*

→	• *rent* = Miete *$ 1500* ***rent*** *a month* = $ 1500 Miete im Monat

1 Sie bezieht eine **Rente** von ihrer alten Firma.
She gets a p________________ from her old firm.

Phrase 1clichés **plump** 1clumsy **Promotion** 1doctorate
Prospekt 1brochures **Provision** 1commission **Reklamation** 1complaint
Rente 1pension

schmal – *small*

→ • *small* = klein
*a **small** pension* = eine kleine Rente

1 **schmale** Gassen um die Kathedrale
n________________ lanes round the cathedral

sensibel – *sensible*

→ • *sensible* = vernünftig
*Now be **sensible**!* = Jetzt sei doch vernünftig!

1 Der Markt reagiert zurzeit sehr **sensibel** auf Preiserhöhungen.
At the moment the market is reacting very s________________ely to price increases.

spenden – *spend*

→ • *spend* = (Geld) ausgeben, (Zeit) verbringen
*I **spent** $200.* = Ich habe $200 ausgegeben.
*We **spent** 2 weeks in Florida.* = Wir verbrachten 2 Wochen in Florida.

1 Wir **spenden** den Erlös wohltätigen Zwecken.
We're don________________ing the proceeds to charity.

stickig – *sticky*

→ • *sticky* = klebrig
***sticky** fingers* = klebrige Finger

1 Ich mache ein Fenster auf. Es ist sehr **stickig** hier drin.
I'll open a window. It's very stu________________ in here.

sympathisch – *sympathetic*

➔	• *sympathetic* = mitfühlend, verständnisvoll *I didn't pass, but everybody was very* ***sympathetic****.* = Ich habe nicht bestanden, aber alle waren sehr mitfühlend.

1 Ich finde den neuen Hausmeister sehr **sympathisch**.
*I find the new caretaker very pleas*________________.

Tablett – *tablet*

➔	• *tablet* = Tablette *one* ***tablet*** *mornings and evenings* = eine Tablette morgens und abends

1 Sie hat das **Tablett** mit den Gläsern fallen lassen.
*She dropped the tr*________________ *with the glasses.*

Warenhaus – *warehouse*

➔	• *warehouse* = Lager(haus) *store goods in the* ***warehouse*** = Waren im Lagerhaus lagern

1 Macy's ist das berühmteste **Warenhaus** New Yorks.
*Macy's is New York's most famous depa*____________ *st*____________.

schmal [1]narrow **sensibel** [1]sensitively **spenden** [1]donating
stickig [1]stuffy **sympathisch** [1]pleasant **Tablett** [1]tray
Warenhaus [1]department store

Korrigieren Sie den durchgestrichenen Ausdruck.

1 Can I ~~become~~ another beer, please?

____

2 What did the ~~chief~~ say when you told him you were leaving the firm?

____

3 I ~~will not come eventually~~, I'm not sure yet.

____

4 The children were no problem, they were ~~brave~~ all evening.

____

5 The new car ~~fabric~~ will provide jobs for 2000 people.

____

6 Damian is a good ~~photograph~~. He works mainly in black and white.

____

7 What do you do for a living? – I'm in the insurance ~~branch~~.

____

8 We had lunch in an old ~~guesthouse~~.

____

9 Tom is very ~~engaged~~ in local politics.

____

10 I must remember to switch off my ~~handy~~ before the concert starts.

____

11 My children are in the sixth class at ~~gymnasium~~.

____

12 I think it's a good idea. What's your ~~meaning~~?

____

13 The hotel you were interested in has sent a ~~prospect~~.

____

14 This timetable is no longer ~~actual~~.

15 KaDeWe is Berlin's most famous ~~warehouse~~.

16 He can't take ~~critic~~. He's always so offended.

17 He took up her breakfast on a ~~tablet~~.

18 You don't find out who the ~~murder~~ is till the last page.

19 On the second train they didn't ~~control~~ our tickets once!

20 The streets round the cathedral are very ~~small~~.

21 I'll leave Jenny a ~~notice~~ so that she knows where we've gone.

22 They are planning a big new advertising ~~action~~.

23 How old does a car have to be before it's ~~an oldtimer~~.

24 Where can I put the ~~map~~ with the letters and photos in?

25 I get a small ~~rent~~ from the state, but it's not enough to live on.

[1]have [2]boss [3]may not come [4]good [5]factory [6]photographer [7]business [8]inn [9]involved [10]mobile (phone) [11]grammar school [12]opinion [13]brochure [14]valid [15]department store [16]criticism [17]tray [18]murderer [19]check [20]narrow [21]note [22]campaign [23]a veteran/vintage car [24]folder [25]pension

1.4 Eins plus eins ist nicht gleich zwei!

Trügerische Zusammensetzungen und Wendungen

Wählen Sie die richtige Entsprechung aus.

Appetit – *appetite*

→ • guten Appetit ≠ ~~good appetite~~

1 Fehlt jemandem noch was? Na dann, **guten Appetit**.
Has everybody got everything? OK then, … .
❑ *eat well* ☒ *enjoy it* ❑ *good meal*

Arm – *arm*

→ • auf den Arm nehmen ≠ ~~*take on one's arm*~~

1 **Nimmst** du mich **auf den Arm**, oder meinst du es ernst?
Are you … , or are you serious?
❑ *holding my thumbs* ❑ *pulling my leg* ❑ *winding me*

Auge – *eye*

→ • unter vier Augen ≠ ~~… *four eyes*~~

1 Könnten wir einmal **unter vier Augen** darüber sprechen?
Could we talk about it … ?
❑ *confidently* ❑ *in private* ❑ *in peace and quiet*

bar – *bar*

→	• (in) bar [Geld] ≠ ~~*in bar*~~

1 Wie zahlen Sie – per Scheck oder **(in) bar**?
How do you want to pay for this – by cheque or … ?
❑ *hard* ❑ *in cash* ❑ *money*

Beruf – *job/profession*

→	• was sind Sie von Beruf? ≠ ~~*What are you in your profession?*~~

1 **Was sind Sie von Beruf**? – Netzwerkadministrator.
What … ? – Network administrator.
❑ *do you* ❑ *do you do for a living* ❑ *work do you have*

Betrag – *amount*

→	• Kleckerbeträge ≠ ~~*… amounts*~~

1 Die Portokosten sind doch **Kleckerbeträge**.
Postage costs are … .
❑ *ground zero* ❑ *peanuts* ❑ *next to nothing*

Bewegung – *movement*

→	• Keine Bewegung! ≠ ~~*No movement!*~~

1 Der Polizist schoss in die Luft und rief „**Keine Bewegung**!“.
The policeman fired into the air and shouted “…”.
❑ *Don't move!* ❑ *Hands up!* ❑ *Stand still!*

Appetit 1enjoy it **Arm** 1pulling my leg **Auge** 1in private **bar** 1in cash **Beruf** 1do you do for a living **Betrag** 1peanuts **Bewegung** 1Don't move!

bewusst – *conscious*

→ • selbstbewusst ≠ ~~*self conscious*~~

1 Tanja ist eine sehr selbst**bewusste** junge Frau.
Tanja is a very self-... young woman.
❏ *aware* ❏ *confident* ❏ *strong*

Beachten Sie: *self-conscious* bedeutet genau das Gegenteil von „selbstbewusst“, nämlich „gehemmt, unsicher, befangen“: *He can't stand up and talk to 200 people, he's much too self-conscious.*

blau – *blue*

→ • ein blaues Auge ≠ ~~*a blue eye*~~

1 Was ist mit dir passiert? Du hast ja **ein blaues Auge**.
What's happened to you? You've got a ... eye.
❏ *black* ❏ *green* ❏ *red*

danke – *thank you*

→ • danke [nein] ≠ ~~*thank you*~~

1 Noch ein Glas Wein? – **Danke**, ich muss noch fahren.
Another glass of wine? – ... , I still have to drive.
❏ *I thank, no* ❏ *No thanks* ❏ *Thanks not*

Daumen – *thumb*

→ • die Daumen halten ≠ ~~*hold your thumbs*~~

1 Ich **halte** dir **die Daumen**. Viel Glück!
I'll … for you. Good luck!
❑ *keep my fingers crossed* ❑ *say seven* ❑ *double my thumbs*

egal – *equal*

→ • egal sein ≠ ~~*be equal*~~

1 **Es ist mir egal**, wo wir uns treffen.
… where we meet.
❑ *No difference* ❑ *I don't mind* ❑ *It's the same*

einbrechen – *break in*

→ • Einbrecher ≠ ~~*breaker in*~~

1 Die **Einbrecher** kamen, als die Familie draußen im Garten war.
The … came while the family was out in the garden.
❑ *burglars* ❑ *criminals* ❑ *thieves*

bewusst [1]confident **blau** [1]black **danke** [1]No thanks **Daumen** [1]keep my fingers crossed **egal** [1]I don't mind **einbrechen** [1]burglars

einziehen – *move in*

→	• Einzugsparty ≠ ~~*moving in party*~~

1 Nächsten Samstag feiern wir unsere **Einzugsparty**. Kommt ihr?
Next week we're having our … . Are you coming?
❑ *housewarming party* ❑ *moving party* ❑ *removal party*

Ende – *end*

→	• Happy-End ≠ ~~*happy end*~~

1 Nicht schon wieder ein Film mit einem **Happy-End**!
Not another film with a … !
❑ *happy close* ❑ *happy ending* ❑ *happy finish*

Entscheidung – *decision*

→	• eine Entscheidung treffen ≠ ~~*meet a decision*~~

1 **Hast** du deine **Entscheidung getroffen**? – Ja. Ich kündige.
Have you … your decision? – Yes. I'm handing in my notice.
❑ *found* ❑ *made* ❑ *done*

erwähnen – *mention*

→	• man braucht nicht extra zu erwähnen ≠ ~~*you don't have to mention extra*~~

1 Dass wir sehr besorgt darüber sind, brauche ich **nicht extra zu erwähnen**.
We are very worried about this, … .
❑ *I don't mention* ❑ *needless to say* ❑ *will be oblivious*

Fall – *case*

→ • für alle Fälle ≠ ~~*for all cases*~~

1 Ich nehme einen Regenschirm mit – **für alle Fälle**.

I'll take an umbrella – … .

❏ *for sure* ❏ *to be certain* ❏ *just in case*

Familie – *family*

→ • Familie Schmitz ≠ ~~*family Schmitz*~~

1 **Familie Schmitz** hat sieben Kinder.

… has seven children.

❏ *The family Schmitz* ❏ *The Schmitz family* ❏ *The Schmitz's family*

Feuer – *fire*

→ • Haben Sie Feuer? ≠ ~~*Do you have fire?*~~

1 Entschuldigung. **Haben Sie** zufällig **Feuer**?

Excuse me. … by any chance?

❏ *Do you have light* ❏ *Have you got a light* ❏ *Can you fire me*

finden, Fund – *find*

→ • Fundbüro ≠ ~~*find office*~~

1 Er bekam seine Prothese am **Fundbüro** zurück.

He got his false teeth back at the … .

❏ *finding office* ❏ *loss office* ❏ *lost property office*

einziehen [1]housewarming party **Ende** [1]happy ending **Entscheidung** [1]made **erwähnen** [1]needless to say **Fall** [1]just in case **Familie** [1]The Schmitz family **Feuer** [1]Have you got a light **finden** [1]lost property office

Freund – *friend*

➔ • Freunde gewinnen ≠ ~~*win friends*~~

1 Nach dem Umzug **haben** die Kinder rasch neue Freunde **gewonnen**.
After our move the children soon … new friends.
❏ *came to* ❏ *made* ❏ *took*

Gast – *guest*

➔ • Gastgeber/in ≠ ~~*guest giver*~~
• Gastfreundschaft ≠ ~~*guest friendship*~~
• Gasthaus ≠ ~~*guesthouse*~~

1 Die **Gastgeber** schienen nur etwa 30% der Gäste zu kennen.
The … seemed to know only about 30% of the guests.
❏ *guestgivers* ❏ *hosts* ❏ *inviters*

2 Ich möchte mich für Ihre **Gastfreundschaft** bedanken.
I would like to thank you for your … .
❏ *hospitality* ❏ *kindness* ❏ *friendliness*

3 In dem alten **Gasthaus** spukt es, sagt man.
People say the old … is haunted.
❏ *pub-house* ❏ *inn* ❏ *restaurant*

Beachten Sie: Das englische *guesthouse* entspricht einer „Pension"!

Geburtstag – *birthday*

➔ • Geburtstag haben ≠ ~~*have birthday*~~

1 Morgen **habe ich Geburtstag**.
… tomorrow.
❏ *I'm born again* ❏ *It's my day of birth* ❏ *It's my birthday*

genau – *exact*

→ • genau genommen ≠ ~~*taken exactly*~~

1 Diese Designänderung ist **genau genommen** ein Vertragsbruch.
This change in design is … a breach of contract.
❑ *examined carefully* ❑ *looked at precisely* ❑ *strictly speaking*

gerade – *straight*

→ • gerade Zahl ≠ ~~*straight number*~~

1 Denk dir eine **gerade** Zahl zwischen 10 und 30.
Think of an … number between 16 and 30.
❑ *equal* ❑ *even* ❑ *pair*

Beachten Sie: das Gegenteil „ungerade Zahl" heißt *odd number*.

Gesellschaft – *company*

→ • Fluggesellschaft ≠ ~~*… company*~~

1 Welche **Fluggesellschaft** ist die sicherste?
Which … is the safest?
❑ *airline* ❑ *flight line* ❑ *flying line*

Freund [1]made **Gast** [1]hosts [2] hospitality [3]inn **Geburtstag** [1]It's my birthday **genau** [1]strictly speaking **gerade** [1]even **Gesellschaft** [1]airline

gesund – *healthy*

→ • der gesunde Menschenverstand ≠ ~~*healthy human understanding*~~

1 **Der gesunde Menschenverstand** sagt einem, dass es so nicht weiter gehen kann.
… tells you that things can't go on like this.
❑ *Common sense* ❑ *Nature* ❑ *Straight sense*

gleich – *the same*

→ • gleich alt/groß ≠ ~~*the same old/big*~~

1 Chefin und Verkaufsleiter sind **gleich alt**.
The boss and the marketing manager … .
❑ *are equally old* ❑ *are the same age* ❑ *have similar age*

2 Die Zimmer sind **gleich groß**.
The rooms … .
❑ *are the same size* ❑ *are equally big* ❑ *have same size*

Grad – *degree(s)*

→ • wir haben 20 Grad ≠ ~~*we have 20 degree*~~ • wie viel Grad haben wir? ≠ ~~*how many … ?*~~

1 **Wir haben über 30 Grad** auf der Terrasse.
… over 30 degrees on the patio.
❑ *It's* ❑ *The thermometer has* ❑ *There are*

2 **Wie viel Grad haben wir** heute?
… today?
❑ *How hot have we* ❑ *How many degrees are there*
❑ *What's the temperature*

gute Nacht – *good night*

➔ • Gutenachtgeschichte ≠ ~~*good night story*~~

1 Sie las Tom eine Gutenachtgeschichte aus *Tausendundeine Nacht* vor.
She read Tom a … from the Arabian Nights.
❏ *bedtime story* ❏ *night story* ❏ *sleep-well story*

halb – *half*

➔ • halb sechs [Uhrzeit] ≠ ~~*half six*~~

1 Wir treffen uns um **halb acht**.
We're meeting at … .
❏ *half past eight* ❏ *half past seven* ❏ *half of eight*

Haus – *house*

➔ • Hausarzt ≠ ~~*house doctor*~~ • Haustür ≠ ~~*house door*~~

1 Dr. Müller ist seit über 20 Jahren schon unser **Hausarzt**.
Dr. Müller has been our … doctor for over 20 years.
❏ *family* ❏ *own* ❏ *personal*

2 Diebe haben die **Haustür** aufgebrochen.
Thieves broke open the … door.
❏ *front* ❏ *home* ❏ *entry*

gesund [1]Common sense **gleich** [1]are the same age [2]are the same size **Grad** [1]It's [2]What's the temperature **gute Nacht** [1]bedtime story **halb** [1]half past seven **Haus** [1]family (in GB auch: GP = General Practitioner) [2]front

herzlich – *hearty*

→ • herzlichen Dank, herzliche Grüße ≠ ~~*hearty thanks, hearty greetings*~~

1 **Herzlichen Dank**. Sie waren mir eine große Hilfe.
… . You've been a great help to me.
❏ *Great thanks* ❏ *Warm thanks* ❏ *Thank you very much indeed*

2 Und **herzliche Grüße** an Ihre Familie!
And … to your family!
❏ *best wishes* ❏ *best greetings* ❏ *tell hello*

Hochzeit – *wedding*

→ • Hochzeitsreise ≠ ~~*wedding …*~~

1 Zehn Tage nach der Hochzeit fuhren sie auf **Hochzeitsreise**.
Ten days after the wedding they went on their … .
❏ *honeymoon* ❏ *kiss-trip* ❏ *nuptual bonds*

Hymne – *hymn*

→ • Nationalhymne ≠ ~~*national hymn*~~

1 Sie haben die falsche **Nationalhymne** gespielt – die von Uruguay, statt von Bolivien.
They played the wrong … – Uruguay's instead of Bolivia's.
❏ *country hymn* ❏ *national anthem* ❏ *national song*

Idiot – *idiot*

→ • idiotensicher ≠ ~~*idiot …*~~

1 „Das ist eine **idiotensichere** Methode“, sagte er. Dann explodierte alles.
“This is a … method,” he said. Then everything exploded.
❑ *fail-safety* ❑ *fool-proof* ❑ *surety*

Inland-, Ausland- – *inland, foreign*

→ • Inlandflug ≠ ~~*inland flight*~~ • Auslandsflug ≠ ~~*foreign flight*~~

1 **Inlandflüge**, Terminal 1; **Auslandsflüge**, Terminal 2.
… flights, Terminal 1; … flights, Terminal 2.
❑ *Domestic … International* ❑ *Internal … External*
❑ *Interior … International*

Jahr – *year*

→ • ein Vierteljahr, halbes Jahr, Dreivierteljahr ≠ ~~*a quarter, half, … of a year*~~ (meist) • 15 Jahre sein ≠ ~~*be 15 years*~~

1 In **einem halben Jahr** wird alles ganz anders aussehen.
In … things will look quite different.
❑ *half this year* ❑ *a half-year* ❑ *six months*

2 Unser Sohn ist jetzt **14 Jahre**.
Our son is now … .
❑ *of age 14* ❑ *14 year-old* ❑ *14 years old*

herzlich [1]Thank you very much indeed [2]best wishes **Hochzeit** [1]honeymoon **Hymne** [1]national anthem **Idiot** [1]fool-proof **Inland** [1]Domestic ... International **Jahr** [1]six months(') (time) [2]14 years old

Kosten – *cost(s)*

→	• auf jds. Kosten ≠ ~~*on sb's costs*~~

1 Wer mitfahren möchte, muss das **auf eigene Kosten** tun.
Whoever wants to go will have to do it … .
❑ *at their own expense* ❑ *on their own expense*
❑ *under their own steam*

kurz – *short*

→	• kürzlich ≠ ~~*shortly*~~ • über kurz oder lang ≠ ~~*… short … long*~~ • in Kürze ≠ ~~*in short*~~

1 „Ich habe **kürzlich**", sagte er, „den Mann im Mond kennen gelernt".
"… ," he said, "I met the man in the moon."
❑ *Briefly* ❑ *Recently* ❑ *Shortish*

2 **Über kurz oder lang** hätten sie die Abteilung sowieso umstrukturiert.
… they would have re-structured the department anyway.
❑ *Earlier or later* ❑ *Sometime soon* ❑ *Sooner or later*

3 **In Kürze** werden wir das Ergebnis haben.
We'll have the result … .
❑ *after short* ❑ *in brief* ❑ *shortly*

leicht – *easy*

→	• leicht fallen ≠ ~~*fall easy*~~

1 **Es fiel mir leicht**, mich zu trennen und die Firma zu verlassen.
… to part company and leave the firm.
❑ *It came easy to me* ❑ *I felt it easy* ❑ *I found it easy*

lesen – *read*

→	• Leseratte ≠ ~~*reading rat*~~

1 Unsere Tochter ist eine richtige **Leseratte**.
Our daughter is a real … .
❑ *bookworm* ❑ *bookeater* ❑ *readaholic*

Lied – *song*

→	• Schlaflied ≠ ~~*sleep … song*~~

1 Tom versuchte es mit einem **Schlaflied**, aber das Baby schrie immer lauter.
Tom tried a … , but the baby cried louder and louder.
❑ *baby song* ❑ *lullaby* ❑ *bedsong*

Linie – *line*

→	• Linienflug ≠ ~~*line flight*~~

1 Fliegen wir mit **Linienflug** oder Charterflug?
Are we going on a … flight or a charter flight?
❑ *quality* ❑ *routed* ❑ *scheduled*

Kosten [1]at their own expense **kurz** [1]Recently [2]Sooner or later [3]shortly
leicht [1]I found it easy **lesen** [1]bookworm **Lied** [1]lullaby **Linie** [1]scheduled

links – *left*

→	• links oben/unten ≠ ~~*left top/bottom*~~

1 Das ist Loch Ness und **links oben/unten** sieht man das Seeungeheuer.
This is Loch Ness and what you can see … is the monster.
❑ *in the left top/below* ❑ *on the top/below left* ❑ *top/bottom left*

Mädchen – *girl*

→	• Mädchen für alles ≠ ~~*girl for everything*~~

1 Wir sind ein kleiner Betrieb und suchen ein **Mädchen für alles**.
We are a small firm and are looking for a … .
❑ *Girl Friday* ❑ *do-it-all person* ❑ *Wondergirl*

mehr – *more*

→	• Mehrwertsteuer ≠ ~~*more value tax*~~

1 Gibt es **Mehrwertsteuer** auf Kinderkleidung?
Is there … on children's clothing?
❑ *add-on-value tax* ❑ *higher-value tax* ❑ *value-added tax*

minus – *minus*

→	• Minus machen ≠ ~~*make minus*~~

1 Die letzte Produktion war so schlecht besucht, dass wir **Minus gemacht haben**.
The last production was so poorly attended that we … .
❑ *did minus* ❑ *lost out* ❑ *made a loss*

Mittel [Arznei] – *medicine*

→	• Schmerzmittel ≠ ~~*pain medicine*~~

1 Es war so schlimm, dass ich **Schmerzmittel** nehmen musste.
It was so bad that I had to take … .
❑ *pain relief* ❑ *pain tablets* ❑ *painkillers*

Natur – *nature*

→	• Naturkost ≠ ~~*nature food*~~

1 Das Gemüse kaufe ich immer im **Naturkost**laden.
I always buy my vegetables in a … shop.
❑ *alternative food* ❑ *health food* ❑ *natural food*

Nummer – *number*

→	• Vorwahlnummer ≠ ~~*… number*~~

1 Haben Sie auch die **Vorwahlnummer**?
Have you got the … , too?
❑ *dialling code* ❑ *pre-dialling code* ❑ *selection*

links [1]top/bottom left **Mädchen** [1]Girl Friday **mehr** [1]value-added tax **minus** [1]made a loss **Mittel** [1]painkillers **Natur** [1]health food **Nummer** [1]dialling code (auch: area code)

Ost(en) – *east*

→	• Die Ostsee ≠ ~~*the East Sea*~~

1 Wir verbringen unsere Ferien dieses Jahr an der **Ostsee**küste.
This year we're spending our holidays on the … coast.
❑ *Baltic Sea* ❑ *Scandinavian Sea* ❑ *Flat Sea*

Paradies – *paradise*

→	• Steuerparadies/-oase ≠ ~~*tax paradise/oasis*~~

1 Er hat sein Geld in irgendeinem **Steuerparadies** versteckt.
He's hidden his money in some tax … .
❑ *haven* ❑ *heaven* ❑ *hole*

parken – *park*

→	• parkende Autos ≠ ~~*parking cars*~~

1 Die Straße war, wie immer zu dieser Tageszeit, voller **parkender Autos**.
As always at this time of day, the street was full of … cars.
❑ *left* ❑ *being parked* ❑ *parked*

Party – *party*

→	• eine Party feiern ≠ ~~*celebrate a party*~~

1 Glenn hat bestanden. Wir wollen **eine Party feiern**.
Glenn has passed. We're going to … a party.
❑ *do* ❑ *have* ❑ *make*

Plus / Minus – ***plus / minus***

→ • im Plus/Minus ≠ ~~*in the plus/minus*~~

1 Ich bin endlich mal wieder **im Plus** / schon wieder **im Minus** bei der Bank.
I'm in the … again at last / in the … yet again at the bank.
❑ *black … red* ❑ *positive … negative* ❑ *credit … debt*

Preis – ***price***

→ • um jeden Preis ≠ ~~*at every price*~~

1 Das müssen wir **um jeden Preis** vermeiden.
We must avoid this … .
❑ *at all costs* ❑ *for every price* ❑ *whatever the price*

privat – ***private***

→ • Privatfernsehen ≠ ~~*private television*~~

1 Die meisten Sportsendungen gibt's im **Privatfernsehen**.
Most sport programmes are on … television.
❑ *business* ❑ *commercial* ❑ *privatized*

Ost(en) [1]Baltic Sea **Paradies** [1]haven **parken** [1]parked **Party** [1]have
Plus/Minus [1]black ... red **Preis** [1]at all costs **privat** [1]commercial

Rede – *speech*

→ • eine Rede halten ≠ ~~*hold a speech*~~

1 Wer wird die **Rede halten**?
Who is going to … the speech?
❑ *do* ❑ *have* ❑ *give*

Risiko – *risk*

→ • ein Risiko eingehen ≠ ~~*enter a risk*~~

1 Wenn wir noch länger warten, **gehen** wir **ein** großes **Risiko ein**.
If we wait any longer, we're … a big risk.
❑ *going* ❑ *making* ❑ *taking*

Ruhe – *rest*

→ • jdn. in Ruhe lassen ≠ ~~*leave sb. at rest*~~

1 Er muss ständig an dem Gerät herumfummeln. Er kann es nicht **in Ruhe lassen**.
He's constantly fiddling around with the machine. He can't … .
❑ *leave it alone* ❑ *let it at rest* ❑ *leave it peacefully*

sagen – *say*

→	• grob gesagt ≠ ~~*… said*~~ • das kannst du laut sagen ≠ ~~*… loud(ly)*~~ • oder besser gesagt ≠ ~~*or said better*~~ • unter uns gesagt ≠ ~~*said …*~~

1 Wir haben **grob gesagt** drei Alternativen.
We have … three alternatives.
❑ *in rough terms* ❑ *roughly spoken* ❑ *roughly speaking*

2 Wir haben viel Geld verloren. – Das kannst du **laut sagen**.
We've lost a lot of money. – You can … .
❑ *say that again* ❑ *shout that out* ❑ *speak that to the crowd*

3 Er konnte, **oder besser gesagt** wollte nicht bezahlen.
He couldn't, or … didn't want to pay.
❑ *actually* ❑ *better* ❑ *rather*

4 Die Qualität war **unter uns gesagt** ziemlich schlecht.
… the quality was pretty poor.
❑ *Between you and me* ❑ *Confidentially*
❑ *Spoken between the lines*

Salz – *salt*

→	• Salzkartoffeln ≠ ~~*salt potatoes*~~

1 Möchten Sie den Fisch lieber mit **Salzkartoffeln** oder mit Reis?
Would you prefer the fish with … potatoes or with rice?
❑ *boiled* ❑ *cooked* ❑ *salt-water*

Rede 1give **Risiko** 1taking **Ruhe** 1leave it alone **sagen** 1roughly speaking 2say that again 3rather 4Between you and me **Salz** 1boiled

sauer – ***sour***

→ • saurer Regen ≠ ~~*sour rain*~~

1 Saurer Regen zerstört die Wälder.
... rain is destroying the forests.
❑ *Acid* ❑ *Bitter* ❑ *Spoilt*

schlafen – ***sleep***

→ • eine Nacht über etwas schlafen ≠ ~~*sleep a night ...*~~ • ausschlafen ≠ ~~*sleep out*~~ • lange schlafen ≠ ~~*sleep long*~~

1 Ich will mich nicht festlegen. Ich will **eine Nacht darüber schlafen**.
I don't want to commit myself. I want to ...
❑ *have a sleep about it* ❑ *sleep on it* ❑ *sleep over it*

2 Morgen habe ich frei und kann **ausschlafen**.
I've got a day off tomorrow and can ... .
❑ *sleep it over* ❑ *sleep in* ❑ *sleep off*

3 Sonntags **schlafen** wir meist **lange**.
On Sundays we usually ... .
❑ *sleep late* ❑ *sleep lately* ❑ *sleep longly*

schmecken – *taste*

→	• Schmeckt es?/Das schmeckt! ≠ ~~*… taste*~~

1 **Schmeckt es?**
… ?
❏ *Do you like it?* ❏ *Does it taste to you?* ❏ *How is your taste?*

2 Herrlich! **Das schmeckt!**
Wonderful. … .
❏ *This is a good taste.* ❏ *This has taste.* ❏ *This tastes good.*

Schmerz(en) – *pain(s)*

→	• Halsschmerzen ≠ ~~*throat pain(s)*~~

1 Ich habe **Halsschmerzen**, ich kann heute nicht singen.
I've got … , I can't sing today.
❏ *a sore throat* ❏ *an inflamed throat* ❏ *throat-ache*

Schnupfen – *cold*

→	• Heuschnupfen ≠ ~~*hay cold*~~

1 Zu dieser Jahreszeit habe ich immer **Heuschnupfen**.
At this time of the year I always have … .
❏ *hay fever* ❏ *hay illness* ❏ *hay sickness*

sauer [1]Acid **schlafen** [1]sleep on it [2]sleep in [3]sleep late **schmecken** [1]Do you like it? [2]This tastes good. **Schmerzen** [1]a sore throat **Schnupfen** [1]hay fever

(Sonnen-)Schein – *(sun)shine*

→	• Mondschein ≠ ~~*moonshine*~~

1 Die Vampire küssten sich im **Mondschein**.
The vampires kissed in the … .
❑ *moonshimmer* ❑ *moonlight* ❑ *nightshine*

Beachten Sie: *moonshine* = „Unsinn“ oder „schwarzgebrannter Alkohol“

schreiben – *write*

→	• einen Test/eine Arbeit schreiben ≠ ~~*write a …*~~

1 Morgen **schreiben** die Kinder wieder eine Englisch**arbeit**.
The children are … another English test tomorrow.
❑ *doing* ❑ *making* ❑ *writing out*

Seite – *side*

→	• Rückseite ≠ ~~*backside*~~

1 Sie können an der **Rückseite** des Gebäudes parken.
You can park at the … of the building.
❑ *back* ❑ *bottom* ❑ *return side*

Sprecher – *speaker*

→	• Nachrichtensprecher ≠ ~~*newsspeaker*~~

1 Der **Nachrichtensprecher** konnte den Namen nicht richtig aussprechen.
The … couldn't pronounce the name properly.
❑ *news announcer* ❑ *newsreader* ❑ *news person*

Steak – *steak*

> → • ein Steak englisch ≠ ~~... English ...~~
> • ein Steak durchgebraten ≠ ~~... through~~

1 Wie soll das Steak gebraten sein: **englisch**, medium oder **durchgebraten**?
How would you like the steak: ... , medium or ... ?
❑ *pink ... cooked* ❑ *rare ... well-done* ❑ *red ... brown*

stehen – *stand*

> → • Standuhr ≠ ~~standing clock~~

1 Sie haben eine wunderschöne, alte **Standuhr**.
They've got a beautiful old ... clock.
❑ *erect* ❑ *grandfather* ❑ *upright*

Stein – *stone*

> → • steinreich ≠ ~~stone rich~~

1 Sein Onkel ist **steinreich**. Halt dich an ihn.
His uncle is ... . Stick with him.
❑ *rich as a sheik* ❑ *Paul Getty V* ❑ *stinking rich*

Sonnenschein 1moonlight **schreiben** 1doing **Seite** 1back
Sprecher 2newsreader **Steak** 1rare ... well-done **stehen** 1grandfather
Stein 1stinking rich

Stück – ***piece***

→	• pro Stück ≠ ~~*per piece*~~

1 Die Stühle kosten $ 420 **pro Stück**.
The chairs cost $ 420 … .
❑ *each* ❑ *individually* ❑ *separately*

Stunde – ***hour***

→	• Sprechstunde ≠ ~~*… hour*~~ • Überstunden ≠ ~~*… hours*~~

1 Hat der Arzt am Freitagnachmittag **Sprechstunde**?
Does the doctor have … on Friday afternoons?
❑ *an appointment* ❑ *patients* ❑ *a surgery*

2 Ich mache keine **Überstunden** mehr. Ich will nicht.
I'm not doing any more … . I don't want to.
❑ *extra time* ❑ *overtime* ❑ *overwork*

Tag – ***day***

→	• am hellichten Tag ≠ ~~*in bright day*~~ • acht/vierzehn Tage ≠ ~~*eight/fourteen days*~~

1 Die meisten Einbrüche geschehen **am hellichten Tag**.
Most burglaries happen … .
❑ *in broad daylight* ❑ *in full day* ❑ *in the middle of the day*

2 Wir treffen uns **in acht Tagen** wieder.
We're meeting again in … .
❑ *a week's time* ❑ *seven daytimes* ❑ *the week*

3 Wir verreisen **vierzehn Tage**.

We're going away for … .

❑ *a fortnight* ❑ *fourteen nights* ❑ *a double week*

Tante – *aunt*

→	• Tante-Emma-Laden ≠ ~~*aunt Emma shop*~~

1 Wir haben einen **Tante-Emma-Laden** gleich hier vorne.

We've got a(n) … just down the road.

❑ *corner shop* ❑ *shop next-door* ❑ *everyday store*

Telefon – *telephone*

→	• ans Telefon gehen ≠ ~~*go to the telephone*~~ • am Telefon verlangt ≠ ~~*demanded on the telephone*~~ • auflegen [am Telefon] ≠ ~~*lay on*~~

1 Kannst du **ans Telefon gehen**? Ich kann gerade nicht.

Can you … the phone? I can't at the moment.

❑ *answer* ❑ *reply* ❑ *take*

2 Frau Wolf! **Sie werden am Telefon verlangt**.

Mrs Wolf! You're … on the telephone.

❑ *asked* ❑ *please* ❑ *wanted*

3 Sie wurde so ausfallend, dass ich **aufgelegt** habe.

She got so abusive that I … .

❑ *finished* ❑ *hung up* ❑ *put it down*

Stück [1]each **Stunde** [1]a surgery [2]overtime **Tag** [1]in broad daylight [2]a week's time [3]a fortnight **Tante** [1]corner shop **Telefon** [1]answer [2]wanted [3]hung up

Treffen – *meeting*

→	• Familien-, Klassentreffen ≠ ~~*... meeting*~~

1 Ich war am Wochenende auf einem **Familien- / Klassentreffen**.
I was at a family/class ... at the weekend.
❏ *encounter* ❏ *renewal* ❏ *reunion*

Turm – *tower*

→	• Leuchtturm ≠ ~~*... tower*~~

1 Ich habe immer davon geträumt, in einem **Leuchtturm** zu wohnen.
I've always dreamed of living in a ... .
❏ *firehouse* ❏ *lighthouse* ❏ *lighting house*

über – *over*

→	• überblicken [abschätzen] ≠ ~~*overlook*~~ • übersehen ≠ ~~*... oversee*~~ • überhören ≠ ~~*overhear*~~ • übernehmen ≠ ~~*overtake*~~ • wenn ich mir das nochmal überlege ≠ ~~*when I consider that again*~~

1 Es ist schwierig, die Lage zu **überblicken**.
It's difficult to ... the situation.
❏ *assess* ❏ *guess* ❏ *register*

2 Entschuldigung, das **habe** ich wohl **übersehen**.
Sorry, I must have ... that.
❏ *remarked* ❏ *overlooked* ❏ *overwatched*

3 Den Gong **haben** wir **überhört**.
We ... the gong.
❏ *didn't hear* ❏ *forgot* ❏ *failed*

4 Kritik **überhört** er einfach.
He just … criticism.
❑ *goes over* ❑ *ignores* ❑ *refuses*
Beachten Sie: *overhear* = „zufällig mitbekommen": *I overheard a conversation at the next table.*

5 Ich brauche eine Pause. Kannst du **übernehmen**?
I need a break. Can you … ?
❑ *attempt* ❑ *replace* ❑ *take over*
Beachten Sie: *overtake* = „überholen": *A Jaguar overtook us at 180 kmh.*

6 **Wenn ich mir das nochmal überlege**, ist der Vorschag ganz gut.
… the suggestion is quite good.
❑ *After further reflecting* ❑ *On second thoughts* ❑ *Reflected*

Uhr – *clock*

→ • Parkuhr ≠ ~~… clock~~

1 Ist die **Parkuhr** abgelaufen?
Has the … expired?
❑ *car parker* ❑ *parking dial* ❑ *parking meter*

Urlaub – *holiday*

→ • Urlauber ≠ ~~holidayer~~

1 600 **Urlauber** sitzen wegen des Streiks der Fluglotsen fest.
600 … are stuck because of the air traffic controllers' strike.
❑ *holidaymakers* ❑ *travellers* ❑ *vacation-makers*

Treffen [1]reunion **Turm** [1]lighthouse **über** [1]assess [2]overlooked [3]didn't hear [4]ignores [5]take over [6]On second thoughts **Uhr** [1]parking meter **Urlaub** [1]holidaymakers

Vater – *father*

→ • das Vaterunser ≠ ~~*the Our Father*~~

1 Viele Kinder können heutzutage noch nicht einmal das **Vaterunser**.
A lot of children today can't even say the … .
❑ *Creed* ❑ *God's Verse* ❑ *Lord's Prayer*

Verkehr – *traffic*

→ • Berufsverkehr ≠ ~~*… traffic*~~

1 Im **Berufsverkehr** werden zusätzliche Züge eingesetzt.
In the … they put on extra trains.
❑ *main times* ❑ *rush hour* ❑ *work travel*

verstehen – *understand*

→ • das versteht sich von selbst ≠ ~~*… understand …*~~

1 **Es versteht sich von selbst**, dass wir die Kosten übernehmen.
It … that we'll bear the cost.
❑ *goes without saying* ❑ *is self-explanatory* ❑ *is as clear as day*

Visite – *visit*

→ • [geschäftliche] Visitenkarte ≠ ~~*visiting card*~~

1 Der Geschäftsführer hat seine **Visitenkarte** da gelassen.
The managing director left his … here.
❑ *business card* ❑ *identification* ❑ *hospitality card*

vor – *before*

→	• vorletzte(r/s) ≠ ~~*before last*~~

1 Davies? Die wohnen im **vorletzten** Haus auf der linken Seite.
Davies? They live in the … house on the left.
❑ *last but one* ❑ *pre-last* ❑ *second*

Wahl – *choice*

→	• eine Wahl treffen ≠ ~~*meet …*~~

1 Ich **habe** meine **Wahl getroffen**. Ich möchte Gold.
I've … my choice. I'd like gold.
❑ *done* ❑ *found* ❑ *made*

was – *what*

→	• was für ein … ? ≠ ~~*what for a … ?*~~

1 **Was für eine** Oberfläche brauchen Sie? Glatt oder geriffelt?
What … surface do you need? Smooth or corrugated?
❑ *in the way of* ❑ *make of* ❑ *kind of*

Vater 1Lord's Prayer **Verkehr** 1rush hour **verstehen** 1goes without saying **Visite** 1business card **vor** 1last but one **Wahl** 1made **was** 1kind of

Wasser – *water*

→	• Trinkwasser ≠ ~~drink water~~

1 Die **Trinkwasser**qualität ist sehr gut hier.
The quality of the … water is very good here.
❏ *drinking* ❏ *feeding* ❏ *drunk*

weg – *away*

→	• Es war weg. ≠ ~~It was away.~~

1 Ich habe die Kamera hier kurz abgelegt und plötzlich war sie **weg**.
I put the camera down for a moment, and suddenly it … .
❏ *disappeared off the face* ❏ *was thin air* ❏ *was gone*

Wohnung – *flat*

→	• auf Wohnungssuche ≠ ~~on flat search~~

1 Tina hat einen Studienplatz bekommen und ist jetzt **auf Wohnungssuche**.
Tina has got a university place and has gone … .
❏ *apartment looking* ❏ *flat-hunting* ❏ *on flat search*

Zahn, Zähne – *tooth, teeth*

→	• die dritten Zähne ≠ ~~the third teeth~~

1 Opa ist so unglücklich. Seine **dritten Zähne** sind ins Klo gefallen.
Grandad's so unhappy. His … teeth have fallen down the loo.
❏ *false* ❏ *replacement* ❏ *wrong*

Zeit – *time*

→	• Zeit kosten ≠ ~~*cost time*~~ • die gute alte Zeit ≠ ~~*... time*~~ • in nächster Zeit ≠ ~~*in the next time*~~ • in letzter/der letzten Zeit ≠ ~~*in the last time*~~

1 Das **kostet** zu viel **Zeit**. So lange können wir nicht warten.
That will ... too much time. We can't wait that long.
❑ *spend* ❑ *need* ❑ *take*

2 In der **guten alten Zeit**, als wir alle Kinder waren, ...
In the good old ... when we were all children ...
❑ *age* ❑ *days* ❑ *years*

3 **In nächster Zeit** werde ich nicht mehr so oft kommen können.
I won't be able to come so often in ... .
❑ *the time ahead* ❑ *the next few weeks* ❑ *the next weeks' time*

4 **In letzter Zeit** habe ich ihn oft gesehen.
I've seen him a lot ... .
❑ *now ago* ❑ *late* ❑ *recently*

zweite(r/s) – *second*

→	• jede(r/s) zweite ... ≠ ~~*every second ...*~~

1 Wir treffen uns jeden **zweiten** Tag.
We meet every ... day.
❑ *alternative* ❑ *odd* ❑ *other*

Wasser [1]drinking **weg** [1]was gone **Wohnung** [1]flat-hunting **Zahn** [1]false
Zeit [1]take [2]days [3]the next few weeks [4]recently **zweite(r/s)** [1]other

Korrigieren Sie den durchgestrichenen Ausdruck.

1 Excuse me, where's the ~~find~~ office? I've lost something.

____

2 I've done lots of ~~overhours~~ this month.

____

3 Our phone number is 24738, and the dialling ~~number~~ is 01460.

____

4 Who is your ~~house~~ doctor?

____

5 I must have ~~overseen~~ that. I'm sorry.

____

6 The wine glasses cost $10 ~~the piece~~.

____

7 Last weekend I was at a class ~~meeting~~ at my old school.

____

8 I'd like my steak ~~fried through~~. I don't like it pink.

____

9 Would you like ~~salt~~ potatoes or rice?

____

10 I spoke to her ~~shortly~~ about this problem. It was only last week.

____

11 The first thing the marketing manager did was to give me her ~~visiting~~ card.

____

12 Is it a ~~line~~ flight, or a charter flight?

____

13 How are you going to pay? – ~~Bar~~.

____

14 There's a car park at the ~~backside~~ of the hotel.

15 ~~We have~~ over 30 degrees in my office. I can't work there.

16 Would you like some more coffee? – ~~Thank you~~. I've had enough.

17 ~~Hearty thanks~~. You've been very helpful.

18 We've had lots of big orders ~~in the last time~~.

19 ~~Private~~ television is financed through advertising.

20 She's young, but very ~~self-conscious~~. She's not afraid of anybody.

21 The ~~newsspeaker~~ got his papers mixed up.

22 I always get ~~hay cold~~ at this time of year.

23 The TV was so loud that we ~~overheard~~ the phone.

24 Which ~~flying company~~ do you usually fly with? Lufthansa?

25 Do you have ~~fire~~?

[1]lost property [2]overtime [3]code [4]family [5]overlooked [6]each [7]reunion [8]well-done [9]boiled [10]recently [11]business [12]scheduled [13](In) Cash [14]back [15]It's [16]No, thank you [17]Thank you very much (indeed) [18]lately/recently [19]Commercial [20]self-confident [21]newsreader [22]hay fever [23]didn't hear [24]airline [25]a light

1.5 Zum Verwechseln ähnlich!

Englische Wortpaare und -gruppen, die man leicht verwechselt

Wählen Sie die richtige Lösung aus.

advice – advise

→ • *advice* = Rat(schlag) [Nomen]
• *advise* = (be)raten [Verb]

1 *Who ❑ adviced / ❑ advised you?*
2 *The ❑ advice / ❑ advise that Tom gave me was completely useless.*
3 *Who ❑ advices / ❑ advises the president in questions like this?*

affect – effect

→ • *affect* = beeinflussen, betreffen [Verb]
• *effect* = Auswirkung [Nomen]

1 *These plans of the management, do they ❑ affect / ❑ effect us too?*
2 *The change will have no ❑ affect / ❑ effect on us.*
3 *We can already see the ❑ affects / ❑ effects of global warming.*

altogether – all together

→ • *altogether* = insgesamt
• *all together* = alle zusammen

1 *How much have we spent ❑ altogether / ❑ all together?*
2 *When was the last time that we were ❑ altogether / ❑ all together?*
3 *You know, I've never seen them ❑ altogether / ❑ all together before.*

at last – at least

→	• *at last* = endlich • *at least* = wenigstens

1 *I've tried to call him ❏ at last / ❏ at least 20 times.*

2 *❏ At last / ❏ At least they didn't throw us out.*

3 *After two and a half hours the plane ❏ at last / ❏ at least took off.*

beside – besides

→	• *beside* = [örtlich] neben • *besides* = neben (= außer), außerdem

1 *There are other reasons ❏ beside / ❏ besides these.*

2 *I want to watch TV, ❏ beside / ❏ besides it's raining outside.*

3 *She sat down ❏ beside / ❏ besides me.*

classic – classical

→	• *classic* = klassisch (= angesehen, von bleibendem Wert, typisch) • *classical* = klassisch (= in Bezug auf Musik, die Antike)

1 *This is a ❏ classic / ❏ classical case of mismanagement.*

2 *I can concentrate better with ❏ classic / ❏ classical music.*

advice 1advised 2advice 3advises **affect** 1affect 2effect 3effects **altogether** 1altogether 2all together 3all together **at last** 1at least 2At least 3at last **beside** 1besides 2besides 3beside **classic** 1classic 2classical

comprehensible – comprehensive

> ➔ • *comprehensible* = verständlich
> • *comprehensive* = umfassend

1 *The handbook must be written in ❑ comprehensible / ❑ comprehensive language.*

2 *We offer a ❑ comprehensible / ❑ comprehensive service package.*

confident – confidential

> ➔ • *confident* = zuversichtlich
> • *confidential* = vertraulich

1 *This information is ❑ confident / ❑ confidential and must remain so.*

2 *Write ❑ "Confident" / ❑ "Confidential" on the envelope.*

3 *We are ❑ confident / ❑ confidential that the present problems can be resolved.*

content – contents

> ➔ • *content* = Gehalt (an etwas) (= Anteil)
> • *contents* = Inhalt (= Enthaltenes)

1 *The fat ❑ content / ❑ contents has been reduced.*

2 *He knew nothing about the ❑ content / ❑ contents of the boxes.*

3 *The ❑ content / ❑ contents of your last letter surprised us greatly.*

currant – current

➔ • *currant* = Rosine
• *current* = laufend, aktuell

1 *Economic growth in the ❑ currant / ❑ current year is very satisfactory.*
2 *I don't like rolls with ❑ currants / ❑ currents.*

desert – dessert

➔ • *desert* = Wüste
• *dessert* = Dessert

1 *Would you like to see the ❑ desert / ❑ dessert menu?*
2 *A new form of management training: crossing the ❑ desert / ❑ dessert on a camel.*

economic – economical

➔ • *economic* = wirtschaftlich (= die Wirtschaft betreffend)
• *economical* = wirtschaftlich (= sparsam)

1 *We have no big ❑ economic / ❑ economical problems at the moment.*
2 *What ❑ economic / ❑ economical policy will the new government follow?*
3 *The new model is very ❑ economic / ❑ economical.*

comprehensible [1]comprehensible [2]comprehensive **confident** [1]confidential [2]Confidential [3]confident **content** [1]content [2]contents [3]contents **currant** [1]current [2]currants **desert** [1]dessert [2]desert **economic** [1]economic [2]economic [3]economical

every day – everyday

> → • *every day* = jeden Tag
> • *everyday* = alltäglich

1 *We have the usual ❑ every day / ❑ everyday problems.*
2 *We have the same problems ❑ every day / ❑ everyday.*

farther – further

> → • *farther* = weiter [nur im räumlichen Sinne]
> • *further* = weiter [im räumlichen und übertragenen Sinne]

1 *We need ❑ farther / ❑ further help.*
2 *Thank you, I have no ❑ farther / ❑ further questions.*

greatly – largely

> → • *greatly* = sehr, höchst, außerordentlich
> • *largely* = größtenteils

1 *The party was ❑ greatly / ❑ largely over when we finally arrived.*
2 *We were ❑ greatly / ❑ largely impressed: they were excellent.*
3 *Reactions varied ❑ greatly / ❑ largely.*

hard – hardly

> → • *hard* = hart, schwer, heftig
> • *hardly* = kaum

1 *But I ❑ hard / ❑ hardly know him!*
2 *We all worked very ❑ hard / ❑ hardly.*
3 *It was raining ❑ hard / ❑ hardly when we came out.*

heading – headline

> → • *heading* = Überschrift
> • *headline* = Schlagzeile

1 *What ❏ heading / ❏ headline do you think I'd find that under?*
2 *The ❏ headings / ❏ headlines in Monday's papers were full of criticism.*
3 *Structure your text more, use more ❏ headings / ❏ headlines.*

heroin – heroine

> → • *heroin* = Heroin
> • *heroine* = Heldin

1 *The ❏ heroin / ❏ heroine of her latest book is a Pakistani immigrant.*
2 *Police have seized at least 6 kilos of ❏ heroin / ❏ heroine.*
3 *The ❏ heroin /*
❏ heroine enters the country along traditional mafia routes.

historic – historical

> → • *historic* = historisch (= bedeutsam)
> • *historical* = historisch (= geschichtlich, aus der Geschichte)

1 *This day is a ❏ historic / ❏ historical day in the history of our nation.*
2 *It was a ❏ historic / ❏ historical decision and changed everything.*
3 *We visited a ❏ historic / ❏ historical museum.*

every day [1]everyday [2]every day **farther** [1]further [2]further
greatly [1]largely [2]greatly [3]greatly **hard** [1]hardly [2]hard [3]hard
heading [1]heading [2]headlines [3]headings **heroin** [1]heroine [2]heroin [3]heroin
historic [1]historic [2]historic [3]historical

homework – housework

> ➔ • *homework* = Hausaufgabe(n)
> • *housework* = Haushaltsarbeit(en)

1 *Who does most of the ❑ homework / ❑ housework, you or your husband?*
2 *I think children should do a share of the ❑ homework / ❑ housework.*
3 *I can't help my son with his maths ❑ homework / ❑ housework – I don't know enough!*

human – humane

> ➔ • *human* = menschlich
> • *humane* = human

1 *Is it ❑ human / ❑ humane to keep animals in zoos?*
2 *It's ❑ human / ❑ humane to make mistakes.*
3 *The ❑ human / ❑ humane body is a wonderful construction.*

imaginary – imaginative

> ➔ • *imaginary* = imaginär
> • *imaginative* = einfallsreich

1 *She's a great designer, she's very ❑ imaginary / ❑ imaginative.*
2 *It's an ❑ imaginary / ❑ imaginative line round the centre of the earth.*
3 *This scenario is completely ❑ imaginary / ❑ imaginative and quite unrealistic.*

industrial – industrious

➔	• *industrial* = industriell, Industrie- • *industrious* = fleißig

1 *This is one of the country's ❑ industrial / ❑ industrious heartlands.*

2 *She's our best engineering student; she's very ❑ industrial / ❑ industrious.*

3 *They're building a new ❑ industrial / ❑ industrious complex west of the town.*

it's – its

➔	• *it's* = es ist (= *it is*) • *its* = sein, ihr

1 *The dog hasn't eaten ❑ it's / ❑ its food.*

2 *I think ❑ it's / ❑ its a pity we can't go.*

3 *Hello? Is that David? ❑ It's / ❑ Its Tom here.*

late – lately

➔	• *late* = spät, zu spät • *lately* = neulich

1 *I haven't seen them very much ❑ late / ❑ lately.*

2 *We arrived ❑ late / ❑ lately because of the bad weather.*

3 *On Sundays I get up ❑ late / ❑ lately.*

homework [1]housework [2]housework [3]homework **human** [1]humane [2]human [3]human **imaginary** [1]imaginative [2]imaginary [3]imaginary **industrial** [1]industrial [2]industrious [3]industrial **it's** [1]its [2]it's [3]It's **late** [1]lately [2]late [3]late

lay – lie

➔	• *lay, laying, laid, laid* = legen • *lie, lying, lay, lain* = liegen • *lie, lying, lied, lied* = lügen

1 *She's ❑ laying / ❑ lying on the sofa.*
2 *I haven't ever ❑ laid / ❑ lain / ❑ lied on a waterbed.*
3 *I'm afraid he ❑ lay / ❑ laid / ❑ lied to you. That's not true.*
4 *He ❑ laid / ❑ lain / ❑ lay the baby back in its bed.*
5 *I don't believe you. You're ❑ laying / ❑ lying to me again.*

loose – lose

➔	• *loose* = lose • *lose* = verlieren

1 *If we ❑ lose / ❑ loose this contract, it will be a disaster.*
2 *Vegetables are usually cheaper if you buy them ❑ loose / ❑ lose.*

major – mayor

➔	• *major* = Major • *mayor* = Bürgermeister

1 *He's retired now. He was a ❑ major / ❑ mayor in the Indian army.*
2 *The ❑ major / ❑ mayor opened the new shopping centre officially yesterday.*
3 *Does London elect its ❑ major / ❑ mayor directly?*

passed – past

→	• *passed* = Form des Verbs *pass* = vergehen, überholen, vorbeigehen an • *past* = vorbei, an … vorbei

1 *We walked* ❑ *passed* / ❑ *past a beautiful old church.*
2 *We* ❑ *passed* / ❑ *past a beautiful old church.*
3 *Sunday* ❑ *passed* / ❑ *past and still no news came.*
4 *The time when I worked 60 hours a week is* ❑ *passed* / ❑ *past.*

precede – proceed

→	• *precede* = vorausgehen • *proceed* = vorgehen

1 *How are we going to* ❑ *precede* / ❑ *proceed? What's the best strategy?*
2 *The results in the* ❑ *preceding* / ❑ *proceeding year were much better.*
3 *The closure was* ❑ *preceded* / ❑ *proceeded by weeks of speculation.*

price – prize

→	• *price* = Preis, den man zahlt • *prize* = Preis, den man gewinnt

1 *The* ❑ *price* / ❑ *prize has gone up 10%. It now costs $385.*
2 *The product got a* ❑ *price* / ❑ *prize in an international design competition.*

lay [1]lying [2]lain [3]lied [4]laid [5]lying **loose** [1]lose [2]loose **major** [1]major [2]mayor [3]mayor **passed** [1]past [2]passed [3]passed [4]past **precede** [1]proceed [2]preceding [3]preceded **price** [1]price [2]prize

principal – principle

→ • *principal* = Haupt-, hauptsächlich, wichtigste(r/s)
• *principle* = Prinzip

1 *The ❑ principal / ❑ principle cause of our problem is the oil price.*
2 *The ❑ principal / ❑ principle cities in the country all have a major airport.*
3 *The ❑ principal / ❑ principle of more money for more work is a fair one.*

raise – rise

→ • *raise, raised, raised* = an-, auf-, hochheben
• *rise, rose, risen* = steigen, an-, auf-, hochsteigen, sich erheben

1 *The rate of inflation has ❑ raised / ❑ risen again this month.*
2 *We last ❑ raised / ❑ rose prices six months ago.*
3 *The rocket ❑ raised / ❑ rose up into the sky.*

receipt – recipe

→ • *receipt* = Quittung
• *recipe* = [Koch-]Rezept

1 *Here's your change. – Can I have a ❑ receipt / ❑ recipe too, please?*
2 *This plan is a ❑ recipe / ❑ receipt for disaster.*
3 *What is your ❑ recipe / ❑ receipt for success?*

shade – shadow

→ • *shade* = Schatten (= schattiger Platz, vor der Sonne geschützt)
• *shadow* = Schatten (= Schattenumriss)

1 *I saw a ❑ shade / ❑ shadow on the wall.*
2 *He always had to live in the ❑ shade / ❑ shadow of his famous father.*
3 *Can we sit in the ❑ shade / ❑ shadow? I don't like sitting in the sun.*

sometime – sometimes

→ • *sometime* = irgendwann
• *sometimes* = manchmal

1 *We must go out for a drink together ❑ sometime / ❑ sometimes.*
2 *I last saw her ❑ sometime / ❑ sometimes last year.*
3 *We meet ❑ sometime / ❑ sometimes for a drink after work.*

stationary – stationery

→ • *stationary* = stehend
• *stationery* = Schreibwaren

1 *The car was ❑ stationary / ❑ stationery for some time before anyone got out.*
2 *We buy all our office ❑ stationary / ❑ stationery online.*

principal 1principal 2principal 3principle **raise** 1risen 2raised 3rose **receipt** 1receipt 2recipe 3recipe **shade** 1shadow 2shadow 3shade **sometime** 1sometime 2sometime 3sometimes **stationary** 1stationary 2stationery

suit – suite

→	• *suit* = Anzug, Kostüm • *suite* = Suite

1 *I didn't need a big conference room, so I booked a ❑ suit / ❑ suite and we met there.*

2 *The company has a dress code: ❑ suits / ❑ suites for men, dresses for women.*

terrible – terrific

→	• *terrible* = furchtbar • *terrific* = gewaltig, toll

1 *I've had a ❑ terrible / ❑ terrific day. One success after another.*

2 *I've had a ❑ terrible / ❑ terrific day: everything went wrong.*

3 *There has been a ❑ terrible / ❑ terrific demand and we're sold out.*

in time – on time

→	• *in time* = rechtzeitig • *on time* = pünktlich

1 *The train left ❑ in / ❑ on time, but arrived late.*

2 *I got there ❑ in / ❑ on time to hear the speech.*

3 *We need the new model ❑ in / ❑ on time for the Bologna Fair.*

used to – be used to

> ➔ • *I used to work* = früher arbeitete ich [immer, aber jetzt nicht mehr]
> • *I'm used to working* = ich bin es gewohnt zu arbeiten

1 *I ❑ used to smoke / ❑ am used to smoking, but I've given up.*
2 *We ❑ used to / ❑ are used to panic situations in this firm.*
3 *I ❑ used to work / ❑ am used to working at weekends. I don't mind it.*

wander – wonder

> ➔ • *wander* = umherirren, bummeln
> • *wonder* = sich fragen, sich wundern

1 *I ❑ wander / ❑ wonder what has happened to him.*
2 *I saw him ❑ wandering / ❑ wondering round Hall 5.*
3 *I ❑ wandered / ❑ wondered if you'd like to meet for a drink.*

suit [1]suite [2]suits **terrible** [1]terrific [2]terrible [3]terrific **in time** [1]on time [2]in time [3]in time **used to** [1]used to [2]are used to [3]am used to **wander** [1]wonder [2]wandering [3]wondered

Übersetzen Sie das Deutsche ins Englische.

1 Do you need any (*weitere*) information?

___

2 The (*Preis*) that she won was worth over $ 10,000.

___

3 Can we sit in the (*Schatten*), please?

___

4 I was sent to an industrial complex in the middle of the (*Wüste*).

___

5 It's (*menschlich*) to make mistakes.

___

6 Our advertising people are very good, very (*einfallsreich*).

___

7 I can't walk any (*weiter*).

___

8 The delivery arrived (*spät*) on Friday afternoon.

___

9 It will cost (*mindestens*) $ 650.

___

10 She always works very (*hart*).

___

11 I (*liege gerade*) on the sofa, watching TV.

___

12 What I've just told you is (*vertraulich*), you understand.

___

13 Prices have (*gestiegen*) again.

___

14 They've (*angehoben*) the price again.

___

15 The building is very old and (*seine*) history is very interesting.

____

16 This is a (*klassisches*) example of a good product that came at the wrong time.

____

17 How much will it cost (*insgesamt*)?

____

18 The new model is very (*wirtschaftlich*).

____

19 The country has big (*wirtschaftliche*) problems.

____

20 Can you (*beraten*) me? I need some (*Rat*).

____

21 How high is the (*Preis*) going to go?

____

22 The (*Inhalt*) of the letter made him laugh.

____

23 I've never (*gelegen*) on such a comfortable bed.

____

24 This is a (*historischer*) day for our country.

____

25 Who does most of the (*Haushaltsarbeiten*) in your family?

____

[1]further [2]prize [3]shade [4]desert [5]human [6]imaginative [7]farther/further [8]late [9]at least [10]hard [11]am lying [12]confidential [13]risen [14]raised [15]its [16]classic [17]altogether [18]economical [19]economic [20]advise, advice [21]price [22]contents [23]lain [24]historic [25]housework

2 Grammatik

2.1 Alles nicht so einfach mit dieser einfachen Form

Einfache Form und Verlaufsform des Verbs

→ Die deutsche Gegenwartsform des Verbs (z.B. **ich lese**) hat zwei verschiedene Entsprechungen im Englischen, die so genannte „einfache Form" (**I read**) und die „Verlaufsform" (**I am reading**). Die Wahl zwischen diesen beiden Formen ist immer wieder eine knifflige Angelegenheit.

1. Einfache Form *(I read)*

Die einfache Form beschreibt etwas, das immer oder immer wieder geschieht bzw. einen Dauerzustand darstellt: berufliche Tätigkeiten, Freizeitbeschäftigungen, Gewohnheiten und Bräuche, allgemeine Tatbestände etc.

I **work** for an American company.
Ich arbeite bei einer amerikanischen Firma.
Don **plays** tennis. *Don spielt Tennis.*
They **get** up later on Sundays. *Sie stehen am Sonntag später auf.*
We **celebrate** Christmas in December.
Wir feiern Weihnachten im Dezember.
It **rains** a lot here. *Es regnet hier viel.*

2. Verlaufsform *(I am reading)*

Die Verlaufsform verwendet man für

a) Vorgänge, die gerade jetzt im Gange sind:

It **is raining** at the moment. *Es regnet (gerade) im Moment.*
I **am watching** TV. *Ich schaue (gerade) fern.*

b) Entwicklungen, die im Gange und noch nicht abgeschlossen sind. Dazu zählen auch Lern- und Ausbildungssituationen:

The company **is growing** fast. *Die Firma wächst schnell.*
Our climate **is changing.** *Unser Klima verändert sich.*
I **am learning / studying** Spanish. *Ich lerne / studiere Spanisch.*
He **is training** to be an actor. *Er macht eine Schauspielerausbildung.*

c) Vorübergehende Situationen, die im Gange und nicht abgeschlossen sind:

She's away. She **is visiting** friends. *Sie ist verreist. Sie besucht Freunde.*
I **am working** from home this week. *Diese Woche arbeite ich zu Hause.*

3. Verben ohne Verlaufsform

Bestimmte Verben verwendet man normalerweise nur in der einfachen Form.

be *sein*
believe *glauben*
belong to *gehören*
cost *kosten*
depend on *abhängen von*
hate *hassen, nicht mögen*
have *haben*
know *wissen, kennen*
like *mögen*
look *aussehen*
mean *bedeuten*
need *brauchen*
own *besitzen*
prefer *vorziehen*
realize *erkennen*
remember *sich erinnern*
see *sehen*
seem *erscheinen*
smell *riechen*
sound *klingen*
think *meinen*
understand *verstehen*
want *wollen*
wish *sich wünschen*

Einige dieser Verben haben jedoch mehr als eine Bedeutung und können in anderer Bedeutung in der Verlaufsform stehen. Vergleichen Sie:

I **have** (~~am having~~) a dog. *haben*
He **is having** breakfast. *essen*

I **see** (~~am seeing~~) the sea. *sehen*
I **am seeing** Ann today. *treffen*

He **looks** (~~is looking~~) ill. *ausssehen*
He **is looking** at some photos. *anschauen*

Ergänzen Sie die einfache Form oder Verlaufsform.

1 My mother-in-law ______________________ with us at the moment. (stay)

2 I ______________________ Spanish. (learn)
I ______________________ it for my job. (need)

3 We ______________________ our holiday. (enjoy)
It ______________________ wonderful here. (be)

4 I usually ______________________ tea for breakfast. (have)

5 I'm sorry, he ______________________ lunch in the canteen at the moment. (have)

6 My wife ______________________ part-time. (work)

7 My son ______________________ to be a designer. (train)

8 We ______________________ cards with friends every Wednesday evening. (play)

9 The number of online customers ______________________ fast. (grow)

10 He has broken his leg and ______________________ from home at the moment. (work)

11 "Soon" ______________________ tomorrow, not next week. (mean)

12 On the telephone she ______________________ younger. (sound)

13 Oh yes, I ______________________ now. (remember)

14 It ______________________ very hot in here now. (get)
We ______________________ a window open. (need)

15 The train usually ______________________ late. (arrive)

Übersetzen Sie.

16 Ein Urlaub in den USA kostet mehr dieses Jahr.

____

17 Es hängt davon ab, ob mein Mann unser Auto benötigt.

____

18 Wir bauen eine neue Lagerhalle.

____

19 Die Situation sieht gut aus. Wir haben genug Zeit.

____

20 Hier schneit es und ich habe eine Erkältung.

____

21 Ich lerne Italienisch.

____

22 Tut mir Leid – er nimmt gerade eine Dusche.

____

23 Unsere Tochter studiert Mathematik.

____

24 Nicht viele Frauen studieren Mathematik.

____

25 Mein Nachbar macht eine Schauspielerausbildung.

____

[1]is staying [2]am learning, need [3]are enjoying, is [4]have [5]is having [6]works [7]is training [8]play [9]is growing [10]is working [11]means [12]sounds [13]remember [14]is getting, need [15]arrives [16]A holiday in the USA costs more this year. [17]It depends (on) whether/if my husband needs our car. [18]We are building a new warehouse. [19]The situation looks good. We have enough time. [20]It is snowing here and I have a cold. [21]I am learning Italian. [22]Sorry – he's just having/taking a shower. [23]Our daughter is studying maths/mathematics. [24]Not many women study maths/mathematics. [25]My neighbour is training to be an actor.

2.2 Dieses *do* ist doch überall

Fragebildung und Verneinung mit do

→ Fragen werden im Deutschen durch Umstellung von **Subjekt** und **Verb** gebildet (z.B. **Er raucht.** – **Raucht er**?). Im Englischen gilt das teilweise auch (z.B. **He is** *a smoker.* – **Is he** *a smoker?*). Teilweise jedoch muss das Verb *do* zur Bildung der Frage herangezogen werden (z.B. *Does he smoke?*).
Auch in verneinten Sätzen (z.B. *Er raucht* **nicht**) kommt das Hilfsverb *do* zum Einsatz (z.B. *He* **doesn't** *smoke*).

1. Fragen

Fragen bildet man im Englischen mit einem Hilfsverb. (Hilfsverben sind Verben, die man zur Zeitenbildung verwendet, sowie Verben wie *can, must* etc.) Ist sonst kein Hilfsverb vorhanden, muss man in der Frage eine Form von *do* verwenden.

	Hilfs-verb		Hilfs-verb		
Ann	**is**	**reading.**	**Is**	Ann **reading**?	*Liest Ann (gerade)?*
He	**was**	**smoking.**	**Was**	he **smoking**?	*Rauchte er (gerade)?*
They	**have**	**eaten.**	**Have**	they **eaten**?	*Haben sie gegessen?*
She	**had**	**arrived.**	**Had**	she **arrived**?	*War sie angekommen?*
Tom	**can**	**help.**	**Can**	Tom **help**?	*Kann Tom helfen?*
I	**must**	**hurry.**	**Must**	I **hurry**?	*Muss ich mich beeilen?*
You	—	**drive.**	**Do**	you **drive**?	*Fahren Sie Auto?*
He	—	**smokes.**	**Does**	he **smoke**?	*Raucht er?*
It	—	**rained.**	**Did**	it **rain**?	*Hat es geregnet?*

2. Verneinung

Sätze verneint man im Englischen mit einem Hilfsverb. Ist sonst kein Hilfsverb vorhanden, muss man eine Form von *do* verwenden.

	Hilfs-verb			Hilfs-verb		
We	**are**	**waiting.**	We	**aren't**	**waiting.**	*Wir warten nicht.*
I	**can**	**come.**	I	**can't**	**come.**	*Ich kann nicht kommen.*
They	–	**know.**	They	**don't**	**know.**	*Sie wissen nicht Bescheid.*
He	–	**smokes.**	He	**doesn't**	**smoke.**	*Er raucht nicht.*
It	–	**snowed.**	It	**didn't**	**snow.**	*Es hat nicht geschneit.*

Korrigieren Sie diese Fragen. Sie haben alle einen Fehler.

1 What means the word "relation"?

____

2 Saw you a ghost?

____

3 Know you their address?

____

4 Speaks he German?

____

5 Did you saw the accident?

____

6 What job do you?

____

7 Where work you?

____

8 When starts the film?

____

9 Does he needs any help?

____

10 Why said she that?

____

Verwandeln Sie diese Sätze in Fragen.

11 You can see the sea.

____

12 The phone is ringing.

____

13 He knows Paris well.

____

14 She has finished breakfast.

____

15 She had breakfast.

____

16 They own the house.

____

17 It will cost a lot.

____

18 They read the *Times*.

____

19 He is reading the *Times*.

____

20 I knew the area well.

____

Verneinen Sie die Sätze 11–20.

____

____

____

____

____

____

[1]What does the word "relation" mean? [2]Did you see a ghost? [3]Do you know their address? [4]Does he speak German? [5]Did you see the accident? [6]What job do you do? [7]Where do you work? [8]When does the film start? [9]Does he need any help? [10]Why did she say that? [11]Can you see the sea?/You can't see the sea. [12]Is the phone ringing?/The phone isn't ringing. [13]Does he know Paris well?/He doesn't know Paris well. [14]Has she finished breakfast?/She hasn't finished breakfast. [15]Did she have breakfast?/She didn't have breakfast. [16]Do they own the house?/They don't own the house. [17]Will it cost a lot?/It won't cost a lot. [18]Do they read the *Times*?/They don't read the *Times*. [19]Is he reading the *Times*?/He isn't reading the *Times*. [20]Did you know the area well?/I didn't know the area well.

2.3 Die verflixten unregelmäßigen Verben

Unregelmäßige Verben I

→ Im Englischen wie im Deutschen gibt es unregelmäßige Verben. Es gibt keine Regel, die einem sagt, welche Verben unregelmäßig sind und wie die Formen lauten – man muss sie schlicht und einfach auswendig lernen.

Grundform	Vergangenheit	Partizip Perfekt	
be	was/were	been	*sein*
become	became	become	*werden*
begin	began	begun	*beginnen*
break	broke	broken	*(zer)brechen*
bring	brought	brought	*bringen*
build	built	built	*bauen*
buy	bought	bought	*kaufen*
catch	caught	caught	*fangen, erwischen*
choose	chose	chosen	*(aus)wählen*
come	came	come	*kommen*
cost	cost	cost	*kosten*
cut	cut	cut	*schneiden*
do	did	done	*tun, machen*
drink	drank	drunk	*trinken*
drive	drove	driven	*fahren*
eat	ate	eaten	*essen*
fall	fell	fallen	*fallen*
feel	felt	felt	*(sich) (an)fühlen*
fight	fought	fought	*kämpfen*

Grundform	Vergangenheit	Partizip Perfekt	
find	found	found	*finden*
fly	flew	flown	*fliegen*
forbid	forbade	forbidden	*verbieten*
forget	forgot	forgotten	*vergessen*
freeze	froze	frozen	*(ge)frieren*
get	got	got	*bekommen*
give	gave	given	*geben*
go	went	gone	*gehen*
grow	grew	grown	*wachsen*
hang	hung	hung	*hängen*
have	had	had	*haben*
hear	heard	heard	*hören*
hold	hold	hold	*halten*
hurt	hurt	hurt	*wehtun*
keep	kept	kept	*weiter (tun)*
know	knew	known	*wissen, kennen*
lay	laid	laid	*legen*
lead	led	led	*führen, leiten*
leave	left	left	*(hinter)lassen; abfahren*
lend	lent	lent	*(aus)leihen*
let	let	let	*lassen*
lie	lay	lain	*liegen*

Ergänzen Sie die richtige Form des Verbs in der Klammer.

1 How many glasses of wine have you __________? (drink)

2 I __________ down in the grass and slept. (lie)

3 We __________ the 6.35 train and __________ to London at 9.55. (catch, get)

4 I've __________ the crossword. I __________ it in 22 minutes. (do, do)

5 They've __________ a big new hotel. (build)

6 I __________ up the pictures last night. (hang)

7 The weather __________, so we __________ a party. (hold, give)

8 I'm sorry, but she's already __________ the office. (leave)

Wählen Sie die richtige Antwort.

9 I'm afraid I've ❑ forgiven / ❑ forgotten your name.

10 He's ❑ bought / ❑ brought a house in France.

11 It ❑ fell / ❑ felt very cold without a pullover.

12 She says she ❑ laid / ❑ lain the papers on your desk.

13 I didn't get wet because Ann ❑ led / ❑ lent me an umbrella.

14 Have you ❑ done / ❑ down that translation yet?

15 We ❑ chose / ❑ choice a lovely warm red colour.

Ergänzen Sie mit einem passenden Verb aus der Liste auf Seite 158 – 159.

16 This year has been a huge success and we've __________ our old record.

17 It __________ last night and there's ice on the roads.

18 He said he was sorry for what he had__________, and I __________ him.

19 He __________ it was a mistake to ask his boss, but he still __________ it.

20 Has the match already __________?

21 The room __________ $ 300 a night.

22 We didn't drive, we __________ because it was quicker.

23 The village has __________ a lot and __________ a small town.

24 Who __________ the car? – My son, because I'd __________ my arm.

25 Before she __________ out, she __________ a note.

[1]drunk [2]lay [3]caught, got [4]done, did [5]built [6]hung [7]held, gave [8]left [9]forgotten [10]bought [11]felt [12]laid [13]lent [14]done [15]chose [16]broken [17]froze [18]done, forgave [19]knew, did [20]begun [21]cost [22]flew [23]grown, become [24]drove, broken [25]went, left

2.4 Noch mehr unregelmäßige Verben

Unregelmäßige Verben II

➔ Auch in dieser Liste wartet manche Überraschung und Fehlerquelle. Doch wenn Sie diesen Abschnitt bearbeitet haben, kennen Sie alle wichtigen unregelmäßigen Verben des Englischen.

Grundform	Vergangenheit	Partizip Perfekt	
lose	lost	lost	*verlieren*
make	made	made	*machen*
mean	meant	meant	*bedeuten; meinen; vorhaben*
meet	met	met	*treffen*
pay	paid	paid	*(be)zahlen*
put	put	put	*stellen, stecken, legen*
read	read	read	*lesen*
ride	rode	ridden	*reiten; fahren*
ring	rang	rung	*anrufen; klingeln*
rise	rose	risen	*(an-, auf)steigen; aufgehen*
run	ran	run	*laufen*
say	said	said	*sagen*
see	saw	seen	*sehen*
sell	sold	sold	*verkaufen*
send	sent	sent	*senden*
shake	shook	shaken	*schütteln*
shine	shone	shone	*scheinen*
shoot	shot	shot	*(er)schießen*

Grundform	Vergangenheit	Partizip Perfekt	
show	showed	shown	*zeigen*
shut	shut	shut	*schließen*
sing	sang	sung	*singen*
sink	sank	sunk	*sinken, versenken*
sit	sat	sat	*sitzen*
sleep	slept	slept	*schlafen*
speak	spoke	spoken	*sprechen*
spend	spent	spent	*verbringen; ausgeben*
stand	stood	stood	*stehen*
steal	stole	stolen	*stehlen*
stick	stuck	stuck	*stecken; kleben*
swim	swam	swum	*schwimmen*
take	took	taken	*nehmen; dauern*
teach	taught	taught	*lehren, unterrichten*
tear	tore	torn	*reißen*
tell	told	told	*erzählen, sagen*
think	thought	thought	*denken*
throw	threw	thrown	*werfen*
understand	understood	understood	*verstehen*
wake	woke	waken	*wecken*
wear	wore	worn	*tragen*
win	won	won	*gewinnen*
write	wrote	written	*schreiben*

Setzen Sie in die Vergangenheit.

1 I (ring) the New York office yesterday.

___

2 I (speak) to Mrs Mailer about it.

___

3 I (think) you knew.

___

4 We (sit) on the floor.

___

5 The journey (take) over 9 hours.

___

6 We last (meet) at the Hanover Fair.

___

7 She (spend) three weeks there last autumn.

___

8 He (write) me an e-mail this morning.

___

9 I (wake) up in the middle of the night.

___

10 He (sleep) for 11 hours.

___

Ergänzen Sie die englische Entsprechung in der richtigen Form.

11 I have __________ this film before. (*sehen*)

12 I __________ it last year in London. (*sehen*)

13 I have __________ my passport. (*verlieren*)

14 He says he's __________ the computer, but it still doesn't work! (*schütteln*)

15 Have you __________ to your boss yet? (*sprechen*)

16 I'm sorry, I don't think I __________ you correctly. (*verstehen*)

17 Someone __________ the documents while I was out of the room. (*stehlen*)

18 The sun __________ at 4.17 that morning. (*aufgehen*)

19 Have you __________ the bill? (*bezahlen*)

20 I haven't __________ so far for a long time. (*schwimmen*)

Ergänzen Sie mit einem passenden Verb aus der Liste auf Seite 162 – 163.

21 I last __________ this dress at Ann's wedding.

22 We drank lots of vodka and __________ some songs.

23 We were __________ out of the restaurant because we were so noisy.

24 I've only __________ 6 days holiday so far this year.

25 I'm sorry, I __________ to tell you earlier.

[1]rang [2]spoke [3]thought [4]sat [5]took [6]met [7]spent [8]wrote [9]woke [10]slept [11]seen [12]saw [13]lost [14]shaken [15]spoken [16]understood [17]stole [18]rose [19]paid [20]swum [21]wore [22]sang [23]thrown [24]taken [25]meant

2.5 Die perfekte Vergangenheit gibt es nicht
Present Perfect *und* Past Tense

> ➔ Im Deutschen sind Vergangenheitsform (z.B. *wir* **redeten**) und Perfekt (z.B. *wir* **haben geredet**) oft austauschbar. Im Englischen ist das nicht so – eine tückische und häufige Fehlerquelle.

1. Deutsch: Perfekt – Englisch: *Past Tense* (Vergangenheit)
Wenn gesagt oder gefragt wird, wann genau (s. Unterstreichungen) ein Vorgang in der Vergangenheit abgeschlossen wurde, muss man im Englischen die Vergangenheitsform verwenden.

*Ich **habe** gestern Tom **gesehen**. / Ich **sah** Tom gestern.*
I **saw** (~~have seen~~) Tom yesterday.

*Sie **haben** letztes Jahr Pleite **gemacht**. / Sie **machten** letztes Jahr Pleite.*
They **went** (~~have gone~~) bankrupt last year.

*Wann **ist** sie **angekommen?** / Wann **kam** sie an?*
When **did** she **arrive** (~~has she arrived~~)?

*Um wie viel Uhr **hat** er **angerufen?** Um wie viel Uhr **rief** er an?*
What time **did** he **phone** (~~has he phoned~~)?

2. Deutsch: Vergangenheit – Englisch: *Present Perfect*

In Verbindung mit unbestimmten Zeitangaben („in letzter Zeit“, „schon (einmal)“ usw.) verwendet man im Englischen das *Present Perfect.*

In letzter Zeit ***hatte*** *er viel zu tun. / In letzter Zeit* ***hat*** *er viel zu tun* ***gehabt.***
He **has had** a lot to do lately.
Warst *du schon einmal hier? /* ***Bist*** *du schon einmal hier* ***gewesen?***
Have you **been** here before?

Im amerikanischen Englisch ist zum Teil – wie im Deutschen – die Vergangenheit möglich. Sicherheitshalber verwende man jedoch bei folgenden Zeitangaben das *Present Perfect*:

already	*schon*
yet?	*schon?* (in Fragen)
always	*schon immer*
before	*schon einmal*
ever?	*schon einmal?* (in Fragen)
so far	*bisher*
not yet	*noch nicht*
never	*nie*
lately	*in letzter Zeit*
recently	*in letzter Zeit*
just	*gerade*

Richtig oder falsch? Wenn der Satz falsch ist, berichtigen Sie ihn.

1 We've met two years ago at the Hanover Fair.

____

2 I haven't been to Canada before.

____

3 I've read the book while I was on holiday.

____

4 It has been easier to learn things when I was younger.

____

5 Yesterday I have had a terrible headache.

____

Ergänzen Sie das *Present Perfect* oder die Vergangenheit.

6 Nearly everybody (check in) now.

____

7 Some people (arrive) last night.

____

8 I (see) the Smiths a few minutes ago.

____

9 It (be) very cold here lately.

____

10 We (go) to the theatre last week.

____

11 We (not be) to the cinema much recently.

____

12 I (write) 15 postcards so far.

____

13 When (you/find) that out?

____

14 I (always/cycle) to work. It's the only exercise I get.

____

15 Ann (phone) at 3 o'clock.

____

16 I (be) in London in April.

____

17 The train (be) very full lately.

____

Übersetzen Sie.

18 Wann ist der Brief gekommen?

____

19 Er ist bei einem Unfall ums Leben gekommen.

____

20 Wir haben uns letzte Woche getroffen.

____

21 Ich war noch nie in Florida.

____

22 Ich wollte schon immer fliegen lernen. Es ist herrlich.

____

[1]falsch: We met … [2]richtig [3]falsch: I read … [4]falsch: It was … [5]falsch: Yesterday I had … [6]has checked in [7]arrived [8]saw [9]has been [10]went [11]haven't been [12]have written [13]did you find [14]have aways cycled [15]phoned [16]was [17]has been [18]When did the letter come? [19]He died in an accident. [20]We met last week. [21]I have never been to Florida. [22]I have always wanted to learn to fly. It's wonderful.

2.6 Seit anno dazumal und immer noch *Present Perfect*

Present Perfect *mit* since *und* for

> ➔ Handlungen, die in der Vergangenheit begonnen haben und bis in die Gegenwart andauern, kann man unterschiedlich sehen – als Gegenwart (z.B. deutsch *ich* **lebe** *hier seit zehn Jahren*) oder als Vergangenheit (z.B. englisch *I* **have lived/have been living** *here for 10 years*). Diese unterschiedliche Sichtweise ist für Deutschsprachige eine häufige Fehlerquelle im Englischen.

1. Deutsch: Gegenwart – Englisch: *Present Perfect*

Anders als im Deutschen verwendet man im Englischen das *Present Perfect,* wenn eine Handlung in der Vergangenheit begonnen hat und bis in die Gegenwart andauert.

Ich ***kenne*** *ihn seit* 1998.*
I **have known** (~~know~~) him since 1998.

Das Auto ***steht*** *seit* über 3 Wochen hier.*
The car **has been** (~~is~~) here for over 3 weeks.

*„seit" + Anfangszeitpunkt (Frage: „seit wann?") = *since*
„seit" + Zeitspanne/Dauerangabe (Frage: „wie lange schon?") = *for*

2. Verlaufsform des *Present Perfect*

Mit der Verlaufsform des *Present Perfect* wird das Andauern der Handlung betont. Bestimmte Verben können jedoch nur in der einfachen Form stehen (s. Übersicht S. 151).

Ich ***arbeite*** *seit 10 Jahren hier.*
I **have been working** here for 10 years.

Ich ***warte*** *schon die ganze Woche.*
I **have been waiting** all week.

Ich ***habe*** *seit einer Woche die Grippe.*
I **have had** the flu for a week.

Test

Ergänzen Sie die einfache Form des *Present Perfect* + *since* oder *for*.

1 The letter (be) ________________ on his desk _____ nearly a week.

2 How long (you/know) ________________ them? – _____ May 2000.

3 I (be) ________________ off work _____ last Friday.

4 They (be) ________________ married _____ over 40 years.

5 _____ last Friday petrol (cost) ________________ 5 cents more.

6 The castle (belong) ________________ to the royal family _____ over 500 years.

Ergänzen Sie die Verlaufsform des *Present Perfect* + *since* oder *for*.

7 We (look for) ________________ somewhere to stay _____ over an hour.

8 I (work) ________________ on this problem _____ yesterday.

9 It (rain) ________________ _____ early afternoon.

10 She (teach) ________________ at this school _____ 1995.

11 They (repair) ________________ this road _____ over a year.

12 I (wait) ________________ for him _____ yesterday afternoon.

13 She (talk) ________________ to the boss _____ nearly two hours.

14 I (learn) ________________ Spanish _____ six months now.

15 We (try) ________________ to repair it _____ 10 o'clock this morning.

Übersetzen Sie. Verwenden Sie die Verlaufsform, wenn das Verb es zulässt.

16 Seit 10 Uhr schneit es.

____

17 Er ist seit mehreren Jahren [schon] tot.

____

18 Wir kennen uns seit über 20 Jahren.

____

19 Ich weiß es schon lange.

____

20 Wie lange warten Sie?

____

21 Ich trainiere Pferde, seit ich 20 bin.

____

22 Ist dieser Baum schon immer hier gewesen?

____

23 Wir besitzen seit zwei Jahren ein Boot.

____

24 Es kostet schon immer mehr im August.

____

25 Ich suche seit Weihnachten eine neue Stelle.

____

[1]has been … for [2]have you known … Since [3]have been … since [4]have been married for [5]Since … has cost [6]has belonged … for [7]have been looking … for [8]have been working … since [9]has been raining since [10]has been teaching … since [11]have been repairing … for [12]have been waiting … since [13]has been talking … for [14]have been learning … for [15]have been trying … since [16]It has been snowing since 10 o'clock. [17]He has been dead for several years. [18]We have known each other for over 20 years. [19]I have known (it) for a long time. [20]How long have you been waiting? [21]I have been training horses since I was 20. [22]Has this tree always been here? [23]We have owned a boat for two years. [24]It has always cost more in August. [25]I have been looking for a new job since Christmas.

2.7 Kein Infinitiv (weder mit noch ohne *to*), sondern *-ing*

Die -ing*-Form (Gerundium) I*

> → Einem deutschen Infinitiv (= Grundform des Verbs) entspricht nicht immer ein Infinitiv im Englischen. Die Verben, bei denen dies der Fall ist, muss man auswendig lernen.

Deutsch: Verb + Infinitiv – Englisch: Verb + *-ing*-Form

Auf bestimmte Verben folgt im Englischen eine *-ing*-Form (Gerundium) – kein Infinitiv.

*Ich **habe aufgehört zu** rauchen.*	I've **given up** smok**ing**.
*Ich kann mir **vorstellen** hier **zu** leben.*	I can **imagine** liv**ing** here.
***Macht es** Ihnen **etwas aus zu** warten?*	Do you **mind** wait**ing**?

admit	*zugeben*	keep (on)	*weiter tun*
avoid	*vermeiden*	like	*gern tun/haben*
carry on	*weiter tun*	love	*sehr gern tun/haben*
consider	*erwägen*	mention	*erwähnen*
delay	*hinauszögern*	mind	*etwas dagegen haben*
deny	*bestreiten*	miss	*vermissen*
discuss	*besprechen*	not help	*nicht umhin können*
dislike	*ungern tun/haben*	practise	*üben*
enjoy	*gern tun/haben*	prefer	*lieber tun/haben*
finish	*zu Ende tun*	recommend	*empfehlen*
give up	*aufgeben, -hören*	regret	*bedauern*
go on	*weiter tun*	risk	*riskieren*
hate	*sehr ungern tun/haben*	start	*anfangen*
imagine	*sich vorstellen*	stop	*aufhören*
involve	*mit sich bringen*	suggest	*vorschlagen*

Ergänzen Sie: -*ing*-Form oder Infinitiv.

1 Did you manage (start) __________ the car?

2 I try to avoid (meet) __________ him at work.

3 But you promised (help) __________ me.

4 She refused (see) __________ me.

5 I suggest (ask) __________ an expert.

6 I don't mind (work) __________ at the weekend.

7 We don't miss (not have) __________ a daily paper any more.

8 I couldn't stop (laugh) __________. It looked so funny.

9 I can't imagine (want) (move) __________. But we'll have to.

10 I've given up (ask) __________ her. She never comes.

11 It seems (use) __________ more petrol than before.

12 He threatened (throw) __________ us out.

13 We'll risk (lose) __________ the contract.

14 He admitted (take) __________ money in return for information.

15 Can't you stop (talk) __________?

16 Where did you learn (ski) __________ so well?

17 I wouldn't recommend (buy) __________ that model.

18 We can't keep (meet) __________ like this.

19 We discussed (buy) __________ a new computer.

20 Have you considered (go) __________ to a hypnotist?

Übersetzen Sie.

21 Ich kann mir nicht vorstellen ohne dich zu fahren.
I can't imagine driving without you

22 Er schlug vor, die Polizei zu holen.
He suggested getting the police

23 Wir konnten es nicht vermeiden, Dreck zu machen.
We couldn't avoid making

24 Wir müssen es üben früher aufzustehen.
We must practise getting up earlier

25 Ich habe nichts dagegen zu warten.
I don't mind waiting

[1]to start [2]meeting [3]to help [4]to see [5]asking [6]working [7]not having [8]laughing [9]wanting to move [10]asking [11]to use [12]to throw [13]losing [14]taking [15]talking [16]to ski [17]buying [18]meeting [19]buying [20]going [21]I can't imagine going without you. [22]He suggested getting the police. [23]We couldn't avoid making a mess. [24]We must practise getting up earlier. [25]I don't mind waiting.

2.8 Weder Infinitiv noch *that*, sondern noch einmal *-ing*

Die -ing-*Form (Gerundium) II*

> ➔ Auf eine Präposition folgt im Englischen grundsätzlich eine *-ing*-Form (Gerundium) – kein Infinitiv oder ein Satz mit *that*.

Präposition + *-ing*-Form

Präpositionen verbinden sich mit Adjektiven, Nomen und Verben zu festen Wendungen, auf die eine *-ing*-Form folgt.

He **is good at** drawing animals.	*Er kann gut Tiere zeichnen.*
Sonia had **the idea of asking** Willi.	*Sonia hatte die Idee, Willi zu fragen.*
We **are thinking of** moving.	*Wir überlegen umzuziehen.*
He **apologized for** not telling us earlier.	*Er entschuldigte sich dafür, dass er uns nicht vorher informiert hatte.*

Adjektiv + Präposition

be **afraid/frightened of** doing something	*Angst (davor) haben, etwas zu tun*
be **capable of** doing something	*fähig sein, etwas zu tun*
be **good/bad at** doing something	*etwas gut/schlecht (tun) können*
be **interested in** doing something	*interessiert (daran) sein, etwas zu tun*
be **proud of** doing something	*stolz (darauf) sein, etwas zu tun*
be **tired of / fed up with** doing something	*es leid sein, etwas zu tun*

Nomen + Präposition

the **advantage/disadvantage of** doing something	*der Vorteil/Nachteil (darin), etwas zu tun*
the **alternative to** doing something	*die Alternative (dazu), etwas zu tun*
the **chances of** doing something	*die Chancen, etwas zu tun*
the **danger/risk of** doing something	*die Gefahr/das Risiko (darin), etwas zu tun*
the **habit of** doing something	*die Gewohnheit, etwas zu tun*
the **idea of** doing something	*die Idee / Vorstellung, etwas zu tun*
the **possibility of** doing something	*die Möglichkeit, etwas zu tun*
the **reason for** doing something	*der Grund, etwas zu tun*
the **thought of** doing something	*der Gedanke, etwas zu tun*

Verb + Präposition

apologize for doing something	*sich dafür entschuldigen, etwas zu tun*
be used to doing something	*daran gewöhnt sein, etwas zu tun*
concentrate on doing something	*sich darauf konzentrieren, etwas zu tun*
decide against doing something	*sich dagegen entscheiden, etwas zu tun*
dream of doing something	*davon träumen, etwas zu tun*
feel like doing something	*Lust (darauf) haben, etwas zu tun*
insist on doing something	*darauf bestehen, etwas zu tun*
look forward to doing something	*sich darauf freuen, etwas zu tun*
object to doing something	*dagegen protestieren, etwas zu tun*
specialize in doing something	*sich darauf spezialisieren, etwas zu tun*
succeed in doing something	*es schaffen, etwas zu tun*
think about doing something	*daran denken, etwas zu tun*
warn against doing something	*davor warnen, etwas zu tun*

Ergänzen Sie: Präposition + *-ing*-Form oder Infinitiv.

1 It's time (go) ________________.

2 I can't get into the habit (get) ________________ up early.

3 I can't go out. I'm afraid (meet) ________________ someone from work.

4 We tried (get) ________________ in through the window.

5 He apologized (come) ________________ late.

6 I hate the idea (throw) ________________ these old things away.

7 Are you interested (come) ________________ with us?

8 What is the alternative (go) ________________ by car?

9 She had the courage (say) ________________ no.

10 We are very proud (win) ________________.

11 What are the disadvantages (live) ________________ in the country?

12 I was impatient (find) ________________ out what happened.

13 I was looking forward (find) ________________ out what happened.

14 Do you ever dream (win) ________________ a lot of money?

15 I asked her (help) ________________ me.

16 There's a big risk (lose) ________________ the contract.

17 He gave us permission (borrow) ________________ his car.

18 Is there a possibility (borrow) ________________ someone's car?

19 I object (use) ________________ throw-away plastic cups.

Übersetzen Sie.

20 Ich bin daran gewöhnt allein zu arbeiten.

____

21 Was waren die Gründe, die anderen nicht einzuladen?

____

22 Ich bin es leid, Ausreden für ihn zu erfinden („machen“).

____

23 Er entschudigte sich dafür, dass er den Termin nicht einhalten konnte.

____

24 Sind Sie daran interessiert, sich einige andere Beispiele anzusehen?

____

25 Wir haben ihn davor gewarnt, in jene Firma zu investieren.

____

[1]to go [2]of getting [3]of meeting [4]to get [5]for coming [6]of throwing [7]in coming [8]to going [9]to say [10]of winning [11]of living [12]to find [13]to finding [14]of winning [15]to help [16]of losing [17]to borrow [18]of borrowing [19]to using [20]I am used to working alone/on my own. [21]What were the reasons for not inviting the others? [22]I'm tired of/fed up with making excuses for him. [23]He apologized for not keeping the appointment. [24]Are you interested in looking at some other examples? [25]We (have) warned him against investing in that firm.

2.9 Wenn nur das Wörtchen „wenn" nicht wäre

if-*Sätze*

> ➔ Aus der Schulzeit weiß es jede(r): *if*-Sätze bereiten immer wieder Probleme – vor allem deshalb, weil „würde", „hätte" und „wäre" oft nicht mit *would, had* und *were* wiedergegeben werden.

Typ 1: Was ist, wenn ...

Bedingung: Gegenwart	**Folge: *will***
If Tom **phones** (~~will phone~~),	I **will** tell him the news.
Wenn Tom anruft,	*sage ich ihm die Neuigkeiten.*

➔ „wenn" im Sinne von „falls" = *if* (nicht ~~*when*~~)!

➔ Kein *will* in der Bedingung – *will* (nicht ~~Gegenwart~~) in der Folge!

Typ 2: Was wäre, wenn ...

Bedingung: Vergangenheit	**Folge: *would/could/might***
If I **won** (~~would win~~) $1 million,	I **would** buy a big house.
Wenn ich ... gewinnen würde,	*würde ich ein großes Haus kaufen.*

➔ Kein *would* in der Bedingung!

Typ 3: Was wäre gewesen, wenn ...

Bedingung: *had-Perfect*	**Folge: *would/could/might* + *have-Perfect***
If I **had left** earlier,	I **would have caught** the train.
Wenn ich früher gegangen wäre,	*hätte ich den Zug erwischt.*

Test

Ergänzen Sie die richtige Verbform.

1 If I knew his e-mail address, I (send) ______________________ him a mail.

2 I'll go without them if they (not be) ______________________ ready soon.

3 What (you/do) ______________________ if they say you can't take the dog with you.

4 Would you go to the USA if someone (offer) ______________________ you a good job?

5 If you (give) ______________________ up smoking, you'd save a lot of money.

6 If I (see) ______________________ her, I would have asked her. But she wasn't there.

7 It (not matter) ______________________ if we had more time.

8 If you (see) ______________________ Ann, will you ask her to phone me, please?

9 I'll do it this evening if I (have) ______________________ time.

10 It (be) ______________________ so easy if we had had the right tools.

11 If I (feel) ______________________ better, I'll go back to work tomorrow.

12 We (move) ______________________ to somewhere bigger if we could afford it.

13 If he had driven more carefully, the accident (not happen) ______________________.

14 We (be) ______________________ back in time if we leave early enough.

15 If he (work) ______________________ harder, he (not have) ______________________ such a bad result in the last test.

16 If I (know) ______________________, I wouldn't have made the suggestion.

17 If I (have) ______________________ enough money, I would have bought it.

18 If we go to New Zealand in June, it (be) ______________________ the middle of the winter there.

19 If you (go) ______________________ to bed earlier, you wouldn't find it so difficult to get up in the mornings.

20 If I (have) ______________________ my mobile phone with me, I could have phoned you.

Übersetzen Sie.

21 Wenn es Samstag regnet, bleiben wir zu Hause.

____

22 Ich hätte angerufen, wenn ich die Nummer gewusst hätte.

____

23 Wenn ich Zeit hätte, würde ich heute Abend ins Kino gehen.

____

24 Ich würde einfach fragen, wenn ich Hilfe bräuchte.

____

25 Es wäre leichter, wenn wir nicht so müde wären.

____

[1]would send [2]aren't [3]will you do [4]offered [5]gave [6]had seen [7]wouldn't matter [8]see [9]have [10]would have been [11]feel [12]would move [13]would not have happened [14]will be [15]had worked … would not have had [16]had known [17]had had [18]will be [19]went [20]had had [21]If it rains on Saturday, we'll stay at home. [22]I would have phoned/called if I had known the number. [23]If I had time, I would go to the cinema/movies this evening. [24]I would simply ask if I needed help. [25]It would be easier if we weren't so tired.

2.10 Mal mit und mal ohne *-ly*

Adjektiv und Adverb

→ Ein Adjektiv sagt etwas über eine Person / Sache aus und beschreibt, wie sie ist, z.B. Sie *ist* sorgfältig. Sie *ist eine* sorgfältige *Mitarbeiterin.* Ein Adverb sagt aus, wie etwas gemacht wird, z.B. *Sie* arbeitet sorgfältig.
Im Deutschen sind Adjektiv und Adverb oft formgleich, z.B. *Sie ist* sorgfältig. *Sie arbeitet* sorgfältig. Im Englischen ist das bis auf einige Ausnahmen nicht der Fall, z.B. *She is* careful. *She works* carefully.

Adverb = Adjektiv + *-ly*

Adverbien werden im Englischen durch Anhängen von *-ly* gebildet.

Ann is **imaginative**. *Ann ist phantasievoll.*
She cooks **imaginatively**. *Sie kocht phantasievoll.*

Ausnahmen:

1. Adjektiv und Adverb formgleich:

daily *täglich*	early *früh*	fast *schnell*	hard* *hart, schwer*
late* *spät*	low *niedrig*	right *richtig*	

*Bedeutungsunterschied beachten:
hard *hart, schwer* – hard**ly** *kaum*
late *spät* – late**ly** *in letzter Zeit*

2. Sonderfall *good – well*

She's a **good** cook. *Sie ist eine gute Köchin.*
She cooks **well**. *Sie kocht gut.*

Gebrauch des Adverbs

Ein Adverb muss verwendet werden, wenn man 1. die Art und Weise einer Tätigkeit oder 2. den Grad einer Eigenschaft beschreibt.

1. Art und Weise – Bezug: Verb

Don drives **dangerously** (~~dangerous~~). *Don fährt gefährlich.*

Ausnahme:
Einige wenige Verben werden nicht mit Adverbien gebraucht:

This pullover **feels soft** (~~softly~~). *Dieser Pullover fühlt sich weich an.*

be *sein*
become *werden*
feel *sich fühlen, sich anfühlen*
look *aussehen*
seem *scheinen*
smell *riechen*
sound *klingen*
stay *bleiben*
taste *schmecken*

2. Grad – Bezug: Adjektiv oder anderes Adverb:

The film was **unusually** (~~unusual~~) long. *Der Film war ungewöhnlich lang.*
He works **incredibly** (~~incredible~~) slowly. *Er arbeitet unglaublich langsam.*

Stellung des Adverbs

Im Gegensatz zum Deutschen kann ein englisches Adverb normalerweise nicht zwischen Verb und Objekt stehen.

I opened the door **quietly**. *Ich öffnete* ***leise*** *die Tür.*

Test

Welche Form ist richtig?

1 Do you know them ❑ good / ❑ well?
2 She works very ❑ slow / ❑ slowly.
3 Listen. This sounds ❑ good / ❑ well.
4 She drives very ❑ careful / ❑ carefully.
5 I don't see them ❑ regular / ❑ regularly.
6 Have you seen Mrs Smith ❑ late / ❑ lately?
7 It's ❑ hard / ❑ hardly quicker by plane, only an hour.
8 I feel ❑ awful / ❑ awfully. We are so ❑ awful / ❑ awfully late.
9 He asked so ❑ nice / ❑ nicely.
10 Do they pay ❑ good / ❑ well?

Setzen Sie die Wörter in Klammern in die richtige Form.

11 It's (cold) ______________________ today, (unusual) (cold) ______________________ today.

12 Tom always works very (hard) ______________________.

13 Mrs Tomkins is an (extreme) (reliable) ______________________ secretary.

14 The new model looks (good) ______________________ and functions (good) ______________________.

15 You can go on a (virtual) ______________________ tour of the museum on the Internet.

16 The deadline is (impossible) ______________________ for us.

17 The music was (wonderful) ______________________ and it was sung (beautiful) ______________________.

18 I don't feel (angry) ______________________, just (terrible) (disappointed) ______________________.

19 This cost an (awful) ____________________ lot.

20 Did you write the address (right) ____________________?

Übersetzen Sie.

21 Gut gemacht, Tom. Sie arbeiten immer so schnell und sorgfältig.

____

22 Sie spricht sehr gut Französisch.

____

23 Wir brauchen schnell ein neues Modell.

____

24 Ich öffnete vorsichtig die Tür.

____

25 Der Vorschlag klingt exzellent.

____

[1]well [2]slowly [3]good [4]carefully [5]regularly [6]lately [7]hardly [8]awful … awfully [9]nicely [10]well [11]cold … unusually cold [12]hard [13]extremely reliable [14]good … well [15]virtual [16]impossible [17]wonderful … beautifully [18]angry … terribly disappointed [19]awful [20]right [21]Well done, Tom. You always work so fast/quickly and carefully. [22]She speaks French very well. [23]We need a new model fast/quickly. [24]I carefully opened the door / opened the door carefully. [25]The suggestion sounds excellent.

3 Präpositionen

Heißt es *at, on* oder etwa *to*?

3.1 Heißt es *at*, *on* oder etwa *to*?
Wendungen mit Präpositionen von A – D

Wählen Sie die richtige Lösung.

Abend – ***evening***

Am Abend hat es geregnet.
It rained … the evening.
❑ *at* ❑ *in* ❑ *on*

Abneigung – ***dislike***

Seine **Abneigung gegen** Katzen ist bekannt.
His dislike … cats is well-known.
❑ *against* ❑ *of* ❑ *with*

Abschluss – ***end***

Zum Abschluss der Tagung gab es eine Theateraufführung.
… the end of the conference there was a theatre performance.
❑ *At* ❑ *In* ❑ *To*

Abwechslung – ***change***

Zur Abwechslung gibt es mal Fisch zum Abendessen.
There's fish for supper … a change.
❑ *for* ❑ *in* ❑ *to*

akzeptabel – ***acceptable***

Ist die Lösung **für** Sie **akzeptabel**?
Is this solution acceptable … you?
❑ *at* ❑ *to* ❑ *with*

allergisch – ***allergic***

Sie ist **gegen** Hunde **allergisch**.

She is allergic … dogs.

❑ *against* ❑ *to* ❑ *with*

Alter – ***age***

Im Alter von 80 Jahren hat sie angefangen zu studieren.

She started to study … the age of 80.

❑ *at* ❑ *in* ❑ *with*

Menschen **in meinem Alter** haben oft Wehwehchen.

People … my age often have little aches and pains.

❑ *with* ❑ *of* ❑ *in*

anders – ***different***

Er ist **anders als** seine Schwester.

He's different … his sister.

❑ *from* ❑ to ❑ as

Angebot – ***offer***

Das haben wir im Moment **im Angebot**.

We've got that … special offer at the moment.

❑ *under* ❑ *in* ❑ *on*

Abend in **Abneigung** of **Abschluss** At **Abwechslung** for **akzeptabel** to **allergisch** to **Alter** at, of **anders** from **Angebot** on

angeln – ***fish***

Er **angelt** ständig **nach Komplimenten**.

He's constantly fishing … compliments.

❑ *after* ❑ *at* ❑ *for*

Angst – ***fear***

Hattest du als Kind **Angst vor** der Dunkelheit?

As a child, were you afraid … the dark?

❑ *at* ❑ *before* ❑ *of*

anklagen – ***accuse***

Er wurde **wegen** Steuerhinterziehung **angeklagt**.

He was accused … tax evasion.

❑ *about* ❑ *for* ❑ *of*

Anteil – ***share***

Wie hoch ist dein **Anteil an** den Kosten?

How big is your share … the costs?

❑ *at* ❑ *in* ❑ *of*

Antwort – ***answer***

Wie lautet Ihre **Antwort auf** die Frage?

What is your answer … the question?

❑ *for* ❑ *on* ❑ *to*

arbeiten – ***work***

Ich **arbeite bei** einer Bank.

I work … a bank.

❑ *by* ❑ *for* ❑ *with*

Art und Weise – *way*

Er lächelt immer **auf** freundliche **Art und Weise**.
He always smiles ... a friendly way.
❑ *in* ❑ *on* ❑ *with*

Arzt – *doctor*

Frau Schmidt ist heute Morgen **beim Arzt**.
Mrs Smith is ... the doctor's this morning.
❑ *at* ❑ *by* ❑ *to*

Assistent(in) – *assistant*

Er ist **Assistent der** Geschäftsführerin.
He's assistant ... the managing director.
❑ *for* ❑ *of* ❑ *to*

aufbrechen – *set off*

Morgen Abend **brechen** wir **nach** Berlin **auf**.
We set off ... Berlin tomorrow evening.
❑ *into* ❑ *for* ❑ *to*

aufteilen – *divide*

Wir müssen den Kuchen **in** fünf gleiche Teile **aufteilen**.
We have to divide the cake ... five equal parts.
❑ *at* ❑ *on* ❑ *into*

angeln for **Angst** of **anklagen** of **Anteil** of **Antwort** to **arbeiten** for **Art und Weise** in **Arzt** at **Assistent(in)** to **aufbrechen** for **aufteilen** into

Auge – *eye*

Sie sind **mit bloßem Auge** nicht erkennbar.
They are invisible … the naked eye.
❑ *to* ❑ *under* ❑ *with*

Augenblick – *moment*

Wie steht der Wechselkurs **im Augenblick**?
What is the rate of exchange … the moment?
❑ *at* ❑ *in* ❑ *on*

Ausblick – *view*

Von oben hat man einen wunderbaren **Ausblick auf** das Tal.
From the top there is a wonderful view … the valley.
❑ *of* ❑ *on* ❑ *onto*

ausprobieren – *try out*

Sie hat es **an** ihren eigenen Familienmitgliedern **ausprobiert**.
She tried it out … the members of her own family.
❑ *at* ❑ *on* ❑ *towards*

Auto – *car*

Wir sind **mit dem Auto** gekommen.
We came … car.
❑ *by* ❑ *in* ❑ *with*

Wir sind **mit** unserem eigenen **Auto** gekommen.
We came … our own car.
❑ *by* ❑ *in* ❑ *with*

Bank – ***bank***

Hat sie viel Geld **auf** der **Bank**?

Has she got a lot of money … the bank?

❑ *at* ❑ *in* ❑ *up*

Bedingung – ***condition***

Ich stimme zu **unter** einer **Bedingung**.

I agree … one condition.

❑ *by* ❑ *on* ❑ *under*

Bedrohung – ***threat***

Was stellt die größte **Bedrohung für** unsere Umwelt dar?

What represents the greatest threat … our environment?

❑ *against* ❑ *at* ❑ *to*

Beerdigung – ***funeral***

Ich war gestern **auf einer Beerdigung**.

I was … a funeral yesterday.

❑ *at* ❑ *by* ❑ *on*

behandeln – ***treat***

Ich werde **wegen** Gicht **behandelt**.

I'm being treated … gout.

❑ *because of* ❑ *for* ❑ *over*

Auge to **Augenblick** at **Ausblick** of **ausprobieren** on **Auto** by, in **Bank** in **Bedingung** on **Bedrohung** to **Beerdigung** at **behandeln** for

Beispiel – ***example***

Das ist ein gutes **Beispiel für** das, was ich meine.
This is a good example … what I mean.
❑ *for* ❑ *from* ❑ *of*

Beleidigung – ***insult***

Die Absage ist eine **Beleidigung für** alle, die sich so eingesetzt haben.
The cancellation is an insult … all who have done so much.
❑ *on* ❑ *to* ❑ *with*

beliebt – ***popular***

Sie ist **beliebt bei** all ihren Kollegen und Kolleginnen ohne Ausnahme.
She is popular … all her colleagues without exception.
❑ *by* ❑ *between* ❑ *with*

beneiden – ***envy***

Ich **beneide** dich **um** deinen schönen Ausblick.
I envy you … your lovely view.
❑ *about* ❑ *over* ❑ *- (= keine Präposition)*

berüchtigt – ***notorious***

Diese Linie ist **berüchtigt wegen** Verspätungen.
This line is notorious … delays.
❑ *about* ❑ *for* ❑ *from*

Beruf – ***profession***

Sie ist nur Amateurjazzsängerin; sie ist Rechtsanwältin **von Beruf**.
She's only an amateur jazz singer; she's a lawyer … profession.
❑ *by* ❑ *for* ❑ *from*

berühmt – ***famous***

Das Restaurant ist **berühmt wegen** seiner Fischgerichte.
The restaurant is famous … its fish dishes.
❑ *for* ❑ *from* ❑ *over*

beschweren – ***complain***

Ich werde mich **bei** der Geschäftsleitung **beschweren**.
I'm going to complain … the management.
❑ *at* ❑ *by* ❑ *to*

Ich werde mich **wegen** des miserablen Service **beschweren**.
I'm going to complain … the dreadful service.
❑ *about* ❑ *against* ❑ *over*

besessen – ***obsessed***

Er ist regelrecht **von** der Idee **besessen**.
He's utterly obsessed … the idea.
❑ *from* ❑ *over* ❑ *with*

besonders – ***special***

Was ist **besonders an** dem heutigen Tag?
What is special … today?
❑ *about* ❑ *over* ❑ *with*

Beispiel of **Beleidigung** to **beliebt** with **beneiden** keine Präposition **berüchtigt** for **Beruf** by **berühmt** for **beschweren** to, about **besessen** with **besonders** about

besorgt – *anxious*

Ich bin **besorgt um** ihre Sicherheit.
I'm anxious … their safety.
❑ *for* ❑ *in* ❑ *over*

bestehen – *consist*

Das Buch **besteht aus** 16 Kapiteln von verschiedenen Autoren.
The book consists … 16 chapters by different authors.
❑ *in* ❑ *of* ❑ *out of*

Besuch – *visit*

Ich war **zu Besuch bei** meiner Tante.
I was … a visit … my aunt.
❑ *to …with* ❑ *on … by* ❑ *on … to*

Bei meinem letzten **Besuch** war es noch schön warm.
… my last visit it was still nice and warm.
❑ *At* ❑ *By* ❑ *On*

beteiligt – *involved*

Sind Sie **an** diesem Projekt **beteiligt**?
Are you involved … this project?
❑ *at* ❑ *in* ❑ *on*

beten – *pray*

Jeden Tag **beten** wir **um** Regen.
Every day we pray … rain.
❑ *about* ❑ *for* ❑ *over*

Bett – ***bed***

Es ist Zeit **ins Bett** zu gehen.
It's time to go … bed.
❑ *by* ❑ *in* ❑ *to*

bewerben – ***apply***

Wie viele haben sich **um** die Stelle **beworben**?
How many have applied … the job?
❑ *after* ❑ *for* ❑ *on*

Bild – ***picture***

Was seht ihr **auf dem Bild**?
What can you see … the picture?
❑ *at* ❑ *in* ❑ *inside*

Die Sonnenblumen sind ein berühmtes **Bild von** Van Gogh.
The Sunflowers is a famous picture … Van Gogh.
❑ *by* ❑ *from* ❑ *of*

bitten – ***ask***

Sie **bitten um** mehr Zeit.
They're asking … more time.
❑ *after* ❑ *for* ❑ *to*

besorgt for **bestehen** of **Besuch** on … to, On **beteiligt** in **beten** for **Bett** to **bewerben** for **Bild** in, by **bitten** for

Blick – *glance*

Sie hat alles **auf einen Blick** erkannt.

She saw everything … a glance.

❑ *at* ❑ *in* ❑ *on*

böse – *angry*

Sie war **auf** mich vielleicht **böse**!

She wasn't half angry … me!

❑ *against* ❑ *on* ❑ *with*

Buch – *book*

Hast du noch andere **Bücher von** dieser Autorin?

Have you got any other books … this author?

❑ *by* ❑ *from* ❑ *off*

Bus – *bus*

Ich bin **mit dem Bus** gekommen.

I came … bus.

❑ *by* ❑ *in* ❑ *on*

Ich bin **mit dem** Nachmittags**bus** gekommen.

I came … the afternoon bus.

❑ *by* ❑ *in* ❑ *on*

denken – *think*

An was **denkst** du gerade?

What are you thinking …?

❑ *about* ❑ *at* ❑ *on*

Oho, dachte ich **bei** mir. Das gibt Ärger.
Oho, I thought … myself. That'll cause trouble.
❏ *by* ❏ *for* ❏ *to*

Dienst – ***duty***

Ich bin **im Dienst**. Ich kann jetzt nicht weg.
I'm … duty now. I can't leave.
❏ *at* ❏ *in* ❏ *on*

Ich bin heute **nicht im Dienst**. Ich habe frei.
I'm … duty today. I've got a day off.
❏ *behind* ❏ *from* ❏ *off*

Diskussion – ***discussion***

Wir hatten eine lange **Diskussion über** die Vor- und Nachteile.
We had a long discussion … the advantages and disadvantages.
❏ *about* ❏ *over* ❏ *with*

diskutieren – ***discuss***

Wir haben lange **über** das Thema **diskutiert**.
We discussed … the topic for a long time.
❏ *about* ❏ *over* ❏ *- (= keine Präposition)*

Blick at **böse** with **Buch** by **Bus** by, on **denken** about, to **Dienst** on, off **Diskussion** about **diskutieren** keine Präposition

Korrigieren Sie die durchgestrichenen Präpositionen.

1 It rained ~~on~~ the afternoon.

____

2 I'm sorry, I have no time ~~in~~ the moment.

____

3 My wife works ~~by~~ a newspaper.

____

4 This model is very popular ~~by~~ women.

____

5 She is allergic ~~against~~ cats.

____

6 Can you give me an example ~~for~~ what you mean.

____

7 The region is famous ~~from~~ its wines.

____

8 I'm afraid he's ~~by~~ the doctor this morning.

____

9 There is something very special ~~on~~ today, can you guess what?

____

10 How much money have we got ~~on~~ the bank.

____

11 I hadn't noticed anything unusual ~~by~~ my first visit.

____

12 I'm afraid ~~before~~ what might happen.

____

13 I think it's time to go ~~into~~ bed.

____

14 They are so small that they are invisible ~~with~~ the naked eye.

15 He is being treated ~~because of~~ shock.

16 The building ~~on~~ the picture, do you know it?

17 He retired ~~in~~ the age of 58.

18 I've never read a book ~~from~~ this author before.

19 We tried the slogan out ~~at~~ 120 people.

20 Can you tell me what the training consists ~~from~~?

21 I was thinking ~~at~~ something larger. Do you have a larger size?

22 I was unable to give them an answer ~~on~~ the question.

23 We discussed ~~over~~ the same question last week.

24 I'm sorry, I'm ~~in~~ duty this weekend.

[1]in [2]at [3]for [4]with [5]to [6]of [7]for [8]at [9]about [10]in [11]on [12]of [13]to [14]to
[15]for [16]in [17]at [18]by [19]on [20]of [21]of [22]to [23]- (keine Präposition) [24]on

3.2 Heißt es *at, on* oder etwa *to*?
Wendungen mit Präpositionen von E – I

Wählen Sie die richtige Lösung.

Ehe – *marriage*

Ich habe einen älteren Sohn **aus** einer früheren **Ehe**.

I have an older son … a previous marriage.

❑ *by* ❑ *off* ❑ *out of*

Ehre – *honour*

Er hielt eine Rede **zu Ehren** seines toten Vaters.

He made a speech … honour of his dead father.

❑ *in* ❑ *on* ❑ *to*

eifersüchtig – *jealous*

Er war immer **eifersüchtig auf** seine berühmte Schwester.

He was always jealous … his famous sister.

❑ *at* ❑ *of* ❑ *on*

Einführung – *introduction*

Das Buch bietet eine hervorragende **Einführung in** das Thema.

The book is an excellent introduction … the topic.

❑ *in* ❑ *on* ❑ *to*

empfindlich – *sensitive*

Dieser Zahn ist besonders **empfindlich gegen** Kälte.

This tooth is especially sensitive … cold.

❑ *on* ❑ *over* ❑ *to*

Ende – ***end***

Gegen Ende des Films wurde es etwas spannender.
It got a bit more exciting … the end of the film.
❑ *against* ❑ *to* ❑ *towards*

Entfernung – ***distance***

Aus dieser **Entfernung** sieht alles sehr klein aus.
… this distance everything looks very small.
❑ *From* ❑ *In* ❑ *Out of*

entscheiden – ***decide***

Für welches Modell haben sie sich **entschieden**?
What model did they decide …?
❑ *at* ❑ *for* ❑ *on*

Entspannung – ***relaxation***

Zur Entspannung gehe ich in die Sauna.
… relaxation I go to the sauna.
❑ *By* ❑ *For* ❑ *To*

enttäuscht – ***disappointed***

Ich war **von** der Resonanz sehr **enttäuscht**.
I was very disappointed … the response.
❑ *from* ❑ *over* ❑ *with*

Ehe by **Ehre** in **eifersüchtig** of **Einführung** to **empfindlich** to **Ende** towards **Entfernung** From **entscheiden** on **Entspannung** For **enttäuscht** with

Erfahrung – ***experience***

Aus Erfahrung weiß ich, dass es ziemlich lange dauert.
... experience I know that it takes quite a long time.
❑ *From* ❑ *Off* ❑ *Out of*

erinnern – ***remind***

Du **erinnerst** mich **an** eine frühere Kollegin.
You remind me ... a former colleague of mine.
❑ *of* ❑ *on* ❑ *to*

Erinnerung – ***memory***

Ich tue es **in Erinnerung an** die schönen Zeiten, die wir zusammen hatten.
I'm doing it in memory ... the good times we had together.
❑ *at* ❑ *of* ❑ *to*

erklären – ***declare***

Irak **erklärte** Kuwait **den Krieg**.
Irak declared war ... Kuwait.
❑ *at* ❑ *on* ❑ *to*

erstaunt – ***surprised***

Über die positive Reaktion war ich sehr **erstaunt**.
I was very surprised ... the positive reaction.
❑ *at* ❑ *from* ❑ *on*

Etage – ***floor***

Sie hat Büroräume **in** der dritten **Etage**.
She has offices ... the third floor.
❑ *at* ❑ *in* ❑ *on*

Euro – ***euro***

Wir haben sie **zu** 30 **Euro** eingekauft und **zu** 50 wieder verkauft.
We bought them … 30 euros and sold them again … 50.
❑ *at* ❑ *on* ❑ *with*

fähig – ***capable***

Vertrau ihm nicht. Er ist **zu** allem **fähig**.
Don't trust him. He's capable … anything.
❑ *at* ❑ *of* ❑ *to*

fahren – ***drive***

Er ist **gegen** die Mauer **gefahren**.
He drove … the wall.
❑ *against* ❑ *in* ❑ *into*

Fahrrad – ***bicycle, bike***

Ich bin **mit dem Rad** gekommen.
I came … bike.
❑ *by* ❑ *on* ❑ *with*

Ich bin **mit Ellens Rad** gekommen.
I came … Ellen's bike.
❑ *by* ❑ *on* ❑ *with*

Erfahrung From **erinnern** of **Erinnerung** of **erklären** on **erstaunt** at **Etage** on **Euro** at **fähig** of **fahren** into **Fahrrad** by, on

Feld – ***field***

Der Bauer stand bewegungslos **auf** dem **Feld**.

The farmer stood motionless … the field.

❑ *at* ❑ *in* ❑ *on*

Fenster – ***window***

Ich kann nicht **bei** offenem **Fenster** schlafen. Es ist mir zu laut.

I can't sleep … . It's too noisy for me.

❑ *by open window* ❑ *with open window* ❑ *with the window open*

Fernsehen – ***television***

Was gibt es heute Abend **im Fernsehen**?

What's … television this evening?

❑ *at* ❑ *in* ❑ *on*

Foto – ***photo***

Auf dem **Foto** ist es Frühjahr.

It's springtime … the photo.

❑ *at* ❑ *in* ❑ *on*

Frage – ***question***

Es tut mir Leid: das kommt **nicht in Frage**.

I'm sorry: that's … question.

❑ *not in* ❑ *off* ❑ *out of the*

fragen – ***ask***

Ich **frage** mal gerade jemanden **nach** der Uhrzeit.

I'll just ask someone … the time.

❑ *after* ❑ *till* ❑ - *(= keine Präposition)*

Frühstück – ***breakfast***

Was trinken Sie **zum Frühstück**?

What do you drink … breakfast?

❑ *for* ❑ *to* ❑ *next to*

Fuß – ***foot***

Wir sind **zu Fuß** gekommen.

We came … foot.

❑ *by* ❑ *on* ❑ *to*

Geburt – ***birth***

Bei der Geburt wog er weniger als 2000 g.

… birth he weighed less than 2000 g.

❑ *At* ❑ *By his* ❑ *On*

Von Geburt ist sie Australierin.

She's Australian … birth.

❑ *by* ❑ *from* ❑ *because of*

Feld in **Fenster** with the window open **Fernsehen** on **Foto** in **Frage** out of the **fragen** - (keine Präposition) **Frühstück** for **Fuß** on **Geburt** At, by

Geburtstag – ***birthday***

Zum Geburtstag bekommt er einen Computer.

He's getting a computer … birthday.

❑ *at his* ❑ *for* ❑ *for his*

Gedanken – ***thought***

Ich fühle mich ganz glücklich **bei dem Gedanken**.

I feel very happy … the thought.

❑ *at* ❑ *on* ❑ *to*

Gedicht – ***poem***

Nenn mir ein berühmtes **Gedicht von** Goethe.

Name a famous poem … Goethe.

❑ *by* ❑ *from* ❑ *of*

Gefahr – ***danger***

Dieser Mann ist eine **Gefahr für** den Weltfrieden.

This man is a danger … world peace.

❑ *against* ❑ *beside* ❑ *to*

Gegenteil – ***contrary***

Im Gegenteil: ich bin ganz deiner Meinung.

… the contrary: I fully agree with you.

❑ *At* ❑ *In* ❑ *On*

geschehen – ***happen***

Was ist danach **mit** ihm **geschehen**?

What happened … him afterwards?

❑ *by* ❑ *to* ❑ *with*

Geschwindigkeit – *speed*

Wir fliegen **mit einer Geschwindigkeit** von 720 kmh.
We're flying … a speed of 720 kmh.
❑ *at* ❑ *above* ❑ *with*

Gesetz – *law*

Nach dem Gesetz müssten sie es abreißen lassen.
… law they should have it pulled down.
❑ *According to* ❑ *By* ❑ *In*

Gesicht – *face*

Du hast noch etwas Marmelade **im Gesicht**.
You've still got some jam … your face.
❑ *at* ❑ *in* ❑ *on*

Gesichtspunkt – *point of view*

Unter diesem Gesichtspunkt wäre es besser zu warten.
… this point of view it would be better to wait.
❑ *After* ❑ *From* ❑ *Out of*

Gesundheit – *health*

Er ist 90 aber noch **bei guter Gesundheit**.
He's 90 but still … good health.
❑ *for* ❑ *in* ❑ *of*

Geburtstag for his **Gedanken** at **Gedicht** by **Gefahr** to **Gegenteil** On **geschehen** to **Geschwindigkeit** at **Gesetz** By **Gesicht** on **Gesichtspunkt** From **Gesundheit** in

Gewalt – *force*

Sie haben die Tür **mit Gewalt** aufgebrochen.

They broke open the door … force.

❏ *by* ❏ *from* ❏ *with*

gewinnen – *gain*

Sie hat durch diese Geschichte **an** Popularität **gewonnen**.

She has gained … popularity through this business.

❏ *at* ❏ *in* ❏ *over*

Glas – *glass*

Ich möchte gern ein **Glas** Rotwein.

I'd like a glass … red wine.

❏ *of* ❏ *with* ❏ *- (= keine Präposition)*

glauben – *believe*

Glauben die Kinder noch **an** dem Weihnachtsmann?

Do the children still believe … Father Christmas?

❏ *at* ❏ *in* ❏ *on*

gleich – *the same*

Es ist **bei** mir genau **das Gleiche**.

It's exactly the same … me.

❏ *by* ❏ *to* ❏ *with*

Glückwunsch – *congratulations*

Herzlichen Glückwunsch zu dem neuen Baby.

Congratulations … your new baby.

❏ *for* ❏ *on* ❏ *to*

greifen – ***reach***

Sie **griff nach** den Sternen.

She reached … the sky.

❏ *after* ❏ *for* ❏ *to*

Grenze – ***border***

Das Haus steht genau **an der Grenze**.

The house is right … the border.

❏ *in* ❏ *on* ❏ *over*

Grund – ***reason***

Wir favorisieren Hermann **aus mehreren Gründen**.

We are in favour of Hermann … several reasons.

❏ *for* ❏ *from* ❏ *out of*

gut – ***good***

Das Gute an dem Plan ist, dass ich persönlich nichts tun muss.

The good thing … the plan is that I personally don't have to do anything.

❏ *about* ❏ *in* ❏ *on*

Janet ist sehr **gut in** Musik.

Janet is very good … music.

❏ *about* ❏ *at* ❏ *on*

Gewalt by **gewinnen** in **Glas** of **glauben** in **gleich** with **Glückwunsch** on **greifen** for **Grenze** on **Grund** for **gut** about, at

haben – ***have***

Wie viel Geld **hast** du **bei dir**?

How much money have you got … you?

❑ *by* ❑ *beside* ❑ *on*

halten – ***stand***

Sie hat immer **zu** ihm **gehalten**.

She has always stood … him.

❑ *by* ❑ *to* ❑ *with*

Hand – ***hand***

Ich schreibe so was lieber **mit der Hand**.

I prefer to write things like that … hand.

❑ *by* ❑ *over* ❑ *with the*

handeln – ***deal***

Er hat **mit** Seidenstoffen **gehandelt**.

He dealt … silk material.

❑ *among* ❑ *in* ❑ *with*

Hass – ***hatred***

Sie sagt, sie empfindet keinen **Hass auf** ihn.

She says she feels no hatred … him.

❑ *at* ❑ *for* ❑ *on*

heilen – ***cure***

Ich bin da**von geheilt**. Keine Zigaretten mehr für mich.

I'm cured … it. No more cigarettes for me.

❑ *from* ❑ *of* ❑ *off*

Heilmittel – ***cure***

Was gibt es für **Heilmittel gegen** Gicht?
What cures are there … gout?
❑ *against* ❑ *for* ❑ *to*

Heirat – ***marriage***

Seiner **Heirat mit** Susanne stand nun nichts mehr im Weg.
There was nothing now to stop his marriage … Susanne.
❑ *of* ❑ *to* ❑ *with*

Himmel – ***heaven***

Am Himmel war kein Stern mehr zu sehen.
There was no longer a star to be seen … the sky.
❑ *at* ❑ *in* ❑ *on*

Im Himmel werde ich dich wohl nicht wiedersehen.
I won't see you again … heaven, I bet.
❑ *at* ❑ *in* ❑ *on*

hindern – ***prevent***

Was **hindert** uns dar**an**, selbst alles zu organisieren?
What prevents us … organising everything ourselves.
❑ *against* ❑ *from* ❑ *to*

haben on **halten** by **Hand** by **handeln** in **Hass** for **heilen** of **Heilmittel** for **Heirat** to **Himmel** in, in **hindern** from

Hochzeit – *wedding*

Ich habe sie **auf der Hochzeit** meines Bruders kennen gelernt.
I met her … my brother's wedding.
❑ *at* ❑ *for* ❑ *on*

hoffen – *hope*

Wir **hoffen auf** gutes Wetter.
We're hoping … good weather.
❑ *for* ❑ *on* ❑ *to*

Höhe – *height*

Die Explosion ereignete sich **in einer Höhe** von 7100 Metern.
The explosion happened … a height of 7100 metres.
❑ *at* ❑ *in* ❑ *on*

hören – *hear*

Ich habe lange nichts mehr **von** ihm **gehört**.
I haven't heard … him for a long time.
❑ *about* ❑ *from* ❑ *of*

Ich habe nie **von** dieser Organisation **gehört**.
I've never heard … this organisation.
❑ *about* ❑ *from* ❑ *of*

Hast du **von** Peters Lotteriegewinn **gehört**?
Have you heard … Peter's win in the lottery?
❑ *about* ❑ *from* ❑ *around*

interessant – ***interesting***

Was ist so **interessant an** diesem Mann?
What is so interesting … this man?
❑ *about* ❑ *in* ❑ *on*

Interesse – ***interest***

Ihr **Interesse an** ihm hat merklich nachgelassen.
Her interest … him has cooled off noticeably.
❑ *about* ❑ *for* ❑ *in*

Hochzeit at **hoffen** for **Höhe** at **hören** from, of, about
interessant about **Interesse** in

Übersetzen Sie das Deutsche ins Englische.

1 You (*erinnerst mich an*) ______________________ an old friend.

2 What's (*im Fernsehen*) ______________________ this evening?

3 The office is (*in der 3. Etage*) ______________________.

4 What do you usually have (*zum Frühstück*) ______________________?

5 The bus (*fuhr gegen*) ______________________ a big tree at the side of the road.

6 Are you (*eifersüchtig auf*) ______________________ your colleague's success?

7 We came (*zu Fuß*) ______________________.

8 What do you want (*zum Geburtstag*) ______________________?

9 (*Auf dem Feld*) ______________________ there is a beautiful old oak tree.

10 What will (*geschehen mit*) ______________________ the building now?

11 The town is (*an der Grenze*) ______________________, not far from Aachen.

12 The weather got better (*gegen Ende*) ______________________ of the holiday.

13 It was designed (*per Hand*) ______________________, not on the computer.

14 She had a beautiful smile (*im Gesicht*) ______________________.

15 Do you (*glauben an*) ______________________ God?

16 He is (*fähig zu*) ______________________ anything.

17 I'd just like a (*Glas Wasser*) ______________________.

18 I can't sleep (*bei offenem Fenster*) ______________________.

19 It was moving (*mit einer Geschwindigkeit*) ____________________ of over 500 kmh.

20 What route did you (*entscheiden für*) ____________________?

21 I think that, (*im Gegenteil*) ____________________, it is a very good idea.

22 Have you got the money (*bei dir*) ____________________?

23 What is so (*interessant an*) ____________________ this story?

24 (*Herzlichen Glückwunsch zu*) ____________________ your new job.

25 We must (*hoffen auf*) ____________________ better weather tomorrow.

[1]remind me of [2]on TV/television [3]the third floor [4]for breakfast [5]drove into [6]jealous of [7]on foot [8]for your birthday [9]In the field [10]happen to [11]on the border [12]towards the end [13]by hand [14]on her face [15]believe in [16]capable of [17]glass of water [18]with the window open [19]at a speed [20]decide on [21]on the contrary [22]on you [23]interesting about [24]Congratulations on [25]hope for

3.3 Heißt es *at, on* oder etwa *to?*
Wendungen mit Präpositionen von J – N

Wählen Sie die richtige Lösung.

jagen – ***hunt***

Die Katze **jagt nach** Mäusen auf dem Dachboden.
The cat is hunting … mice in the attic.
❑ *after* ❑ *at* ❑ *for*

Jahr – ***year***

Mit 58 **Jahren** hat sie ein Studium angefangen.
She started to study … .
❑ *at 58 years* ❑ *at the age of 58* ❑ *with 58 years*

Kampf – ***fight***

Bonzo hat sich **bei einem Kampf** mit einem anderen Hund verletzt.
Bonzo got hurt … a fight with another dog.
❑ *by* ❑ *in* ❑ *over*

Karte – ***map***

Laut Karte müssten wir bald da sein.
… map we should soon be there.
❑ *According* ❑ *According to the* ❑ *By the*

Kino – ***cinema***

Wir waren gestern Abend **im Kino**.
We were … the cinema last night.
❑ *at* ❑ *in* ❑ *to*

kleben – ***stick***

Mein Nachbar hat einen Zettel **an** meine Tür **geklebt**.

My neighbour stuck a note … my door.

❑ *against* ❑ *at* ❑ *to*

kommentieren – ***comment***

Ich habe deinen Redetext **kommentiert** – er liegt auf deinem Schreibtisch.

I've commented … your speech text – it's on your desk.

❑ *on* ❑ *to* ❑ *- (= keine Präposition)*

Konto – ***account***

Wie viel Geld haben wir momentan **auf dem Konto**?

How much money have we got … the account at the moment?

❑ *at* ❑ *in* ❑ *on*

Ich habe ein **Konto bei** einer Online-Bank.

I've got an account … an online bank.

❑ *at* ❑ *in* ❑ *with*

Wir müssen etwas **auf das Konto** einzahlen.

We've got to pay some money … the account.

❑ *into* ❑ *on* ❑ *onto*

jagen for **Jahr** at the age of 58 **Kampf** in **Karte** According to the **Kino** at **kleben** to **kommentieren** on **Konto** in, with, into

Konzert – ***concert***

Wir waren gestern Abend **auf einem Konzert**.

We were … a concert yesterday evening.

❑ *at* ❑ *by* ❑ *on*

Kreditkarte – ***credit card***

Ich zahle **mit Kreditkarte**.

I'll pay … credit card.

❑ *by* ❑ *through* ❑ *with*

kritisch – ***critical***

Ich stehe dem Vorschlag **kritisch gegenüber**.

I'm critical … the suggestion.

❑ *from* ❑ *of* ❑ *to*

Küste – ***coast***

Wir wohnen **an der Küste**.

We live … the coast.

❑ *against* ❑ *next to* ❑ *on*

Die Abtei liegt auf einer kleinen Insel **vor der Küste**.

The abbey is on a small island … the coast.

❑ *before* ❑ *by* ❑ *off*

lachen – ***laugh***

Es ist unfair, ihn **wegen** seines Akzents **auszulachen**.

It's unfair to laugh … him because of his accent.

❑ *against* ❑ *at* ❑ *on*

Hinterher konnte ich **darüber lachen**.
Afterwards I was able to laugh ... it.
❑ *about* ❑ *from* ❑ *on*

Lager – ***stock***

Diesen Artikel haben wir zurzeit nicht **auf Lager**.
We haven't got this article ... stock at the moment.
❑ *inside* ❑ *in* ❑ *on*

Land – ***country***

Sie wohnen in einem Dorf **auf dem Land**.
They live in a village ... the country.
❑ *at* ❑ *in* ❑ *on*

laufen – ***run***

Der Hund ist mir **hinterher gelaufen**.
The dog ran ... me.
❑ *after* ❑ *behind* ❑ *beyond*

Konzert at **Kreditkarte** by **kritisch** of **Küste** on, off **lachen** at, at **Lager** in **Land** in **laufen** after

leben – *live*

Von $400 im Monat kann man nicht **leben**.
You can't live … $400 a month.
❏ *by* ❏ *from* ❏ *on*

Er **lebt von** seinen Ersparnissen.
He lives … his savings.
❏ *by* ❏ *from* ❏ *off*

lebenswichtig – *vital*

Diese Entscheidung ist **für** uns **lebenswichtig**.
This decision is vital … us.
❏ *by* ❏ *to* ❏ *with*

Leid – *sorry*

Es tut mir **Leid um** die Kinder.
I feel sorry … the children.
❏ *among* ❏ *for* ❏ *over*

leiden – *suffer*

Er **leidet an** Asthma.
He suffers … asthma.
❏ *from* ❏ *of* ❏ *off*

lernen – *learn*

Kann man wirklich **aus** seinen **Fehlern** lernen?
Can people really learn … their mistakes?
❏ *from* ❏ *off* ❏ *out of*

Liebe – *love*

Seine **Liebe zu** ihr war größer als seine Liebe zum Geld.
His love ... her was stronger than his love of money.

❑ *after* ❑ *for* ❑ *to*

Er hat nicht **aus Liebe** geheiratet.
He didn't marry ... love.

❑ *by* ❑ *for* ❑ *over*

Lied – *song*

Von wem ist dieses **Lied**?
Who is the song ...?

❑ *by* ❑ *from* ❑ *of*

links – *left*

Wir wohnen **links von** der Kirche.
We live ... the church.

❑ *in the left of* ❑ *left from* ❑ *to the left of*

Luftpost – *air mail*

Ich möchte das Paket **per Luftpost** verschicken.
I'd like to send the parcel ... air mail.

❑ *by* ❑ *per* ❑ *with*

leben on, off **lebenswichtig** to **Leid** for **leiden** from **lernen** from **Liebe** for, for **Lied** by **links** to the left of **Luftpost** by

Mal – ***time***

Diese Reise mache ich jetzt **zum** achten **Mal**.

I'm doing this journey now … the eighth time.

❑ *at* ❑ *for* ❑ *to*

Mangel – ***lack***

Wir mussten **aus Mangel an** Zeit aufgeben.

We had to give up … time.

❑ *for lack of* ❑ *from lack of* ❑ *under lack from*

Mantel – ***coat***

Wer ist diese Dame **mit** dem roten **Mantel**?

Who's that lady … the red coat.

❑ *by* ❑ *in* ❑ *under*

Markt – ***market***

Unser Gemüse kaufen wir immer **auf dem Markt**.

We always buy our vegetables … the market.

❑ *at* ❑ *by* ❑ *down*

Meer – ***sea***

Ich wohne gern **am Meer**.

I like living … the sea.

❑ *at* ❑ *by* ❑ *on*

meinen – ***mean***

Was hat sie **mit** „kostengünstig“ genau **gemeint**?

What did she mean exactly … "cheaply"?

❑ *by* ❑ *through* ❑ *with*

Meinung – ***opinion***

Meiner **Meinung nach** essen wir alle zu viel.
… my opinion we all eat too much.
❑ *According to* ❑ *By* ❑ *In*

Militär – ***army***

Unser Sohn ist zurzeit **beim Militär**.
Our son is … the army at present.
❑ *at* ❑ *by* ❑ *in*

Minute – ***minute***

Wir haben **in letzter Minute** gebucht.
We booked … the last minute.
❑ *at* ❑ *in* ❑ *on*

misstrauisch – ***suspicious***

Ich bin **misstrauisch gegenüber** seinen Absichten.
I'm suspicious … his intentions.
❑ *at* ❑ *of* ❑ *towards*

Mitglied – ***member***

Ich bin **Mitglied in** einem Schachklub.
I'm … a chess club.
❑ *a member in* ❑ *a member of* ❑ *member in*

Mal for **Mangel** for lack of **Mantel** in **Markt** at **Meer** by **meinen** by **Meinung** In **Militär** in **Minute** at **misstrauisch** of **Mitglied** a member of

multiplizieren – ***multiply***

Jetzt müssen wir noch das Ergebnis **mit** sechs **multiplizieren**.

And now we have to multiply the result … six.

❏ *by* ❏ *about* ❏ *with*

Musik – ***music***

Das ist **Musik in meinen Ohren**.

That's music … my ears.

❏ *in* ❏ *into* ❏ *to*

Nachrichten – ***news***

Das habe ich **in den Nachrichten** gehört.

I heard it … the news.

❏ *at* ❏ *by* ❏ *on*

Name – ***name***

Ich kenne sie **dem Namen nach**.

I know her … name.

❏ *according to* ❏ *after* ❏ *by*

Kennen Sie einen Ort **mit dem Namen** *Slaughter*?

Do you know a place … Slaughter?

❏ *by the name of* ❏ *by name* ❏ *with name*

Natur – ***nature***

Diese Tiere sind **von Natur aus** scheu.

These animals are shy … nature.

❏ *by* ❏ *from* ❏ *out of*

Neid – ***envy***

Sie waren alle **gelb vor Neid**.

They were all green [!] ... envy.

❑ *for* ❑ *from* ❑ *with*

Neujahr – ***New Year***

Zu Neujahr wollen wir dann verreisen.

And then ... New Year we want to go away.

❑ *at* ❑ *in* ❑ *on*

Nostalgie – ***nostalgia***

Der Geruch weckte **Nostagie nach** längst vergangenen Zeiten.

The smell aroused nostalgia ... times long since past.

❑ *at* ❑ *for* ❑ *of*

Null – ***zero***

Es sind drei Grad **über/unter Null**.

It is [!] three degrees ... zero.

❑ *above/below* ❑ *over/under* ❑ *above/under*

Nummer – ***number***

Ruf mich **unter dieser Nummer** an.

Call me ... this number.

❑ *at* ❑ *by* ❑ *under*

mutiplizieren by **Musik** to **Nachrichten** on **Name** by, by the name of **Natur** by **Neid** with **Neujahr** at **Nostalgie** for **Null** above/below **Nummer** at

Korrigieren Sie die durchgestrichenen Präpositionen.

1 We went ~~in~~ ___________ the movies yesterday evening.

2 Tonight we're going ~~in~~ ___________ a jazz concert.

3 It's an old song ~~from~~ ___________ the Beatles.

4 He suffers ~~on~~ ___________ bad headaches.

5 It's a nice little town ~~at~~ ___________ the coast.

6 It won't stick ~~at~~ ___________ this surface.

7 I'll pay ~~with~~ ___________ credit card, please.

8 Multiply the production costs ~~with~~ ___________ six and you've got the selling price.

9 How long have you been a member ~~in~~ ___________ this orchestra?

10 I don't think I'd like to live ~~on~~ ___________ the country.

11 Afterwards I was able to laugh ~~over~~ ___________ it.

12 We made our decision ~~in~~ ___________ the last minute.

13 We nearly always spend our holidays ~~on~~ ___________ the sea.

14 She started to learn to dance ~~in~~ ___________ the age of three.

15 Have you heard of a product ~~with~~ ___________ the name of Prosleep?

16 The museum is to the left ~~in~~ ___________ the town hall.

17 She was green ~~for~~ ___________ envy when I told her.

18 They invested the money and lived ~~from~~ ___________ the interest.

19 It's only 1 degree ~~over~~ ___________ zero here, and it's snowing.

20 Do people really learn ~~off~~ ___________ their mistakes?

21 Their son is a major ~~by~~ ___________ the army.

22 How much money will be left ~~on~~ ___________ our bank account after we've paid?

23 What do you mean ~~with~~ ___________ "soon"?

24 You can reach me ~~under~~ ___________ this number: 01470 25083.

25 Sorry, we don't have that model ~~on~~ ___________ stock at the moment.

[1]to [2]to [3]by [4]from [5]by/on [6]on [7]by [8]by [9]of [10]in [11]about [12]at [13]by [14]at [15]by [16]of [17]with [18]off [19]above [20]from [21]in [22]in [23]by [24]at [25]in

3.4 Heißt es *at*, *on* oder etwa *to*?
Wendungen mit Präpositionen von O – S

Wählen Sie die richtige Lösung.

offensichtlich – ***obvious***

Es war **offensichtlich für** jeden, der die Entwicklung der Firma verfolgt hatte.
It was obvious … anyone who had followed the firm's development.
❑ *from* ❑ *on* ❑ *to*

ordnen – ***arrange***

Wir **ordnen** die Bücher **nach** Alter.
We'll arrange the books … age.
❑ *after* ❑ *by* ❑ *from*

Ostern – ***Easter***

Zu Ostern bleiben wir zu Hause.
We're staying at home … Easter.
❑ *at* ❑ *in* ❑ *on*

passen – ***go***

Die Schuhe **passen** nicht **zu** dem Kleid.
The shoes don't go … the dress.
❑ *on* ❑ *to* ❑ *with*

Plan – ***plan***

Alles läuft **nach Plan**.
Everything is going … plan.
❑ *according to* ❑ *by* ❑ *on*

Platz – ***place***

Ist nun alles **am** richtigen **Platz**?

Now, is everything … the right place?

❑ *at* ❑ *in* ❑ *on*

Polizeiwache – ***police station***

Sie hielten ihn **auf der Polizeiwache** fest.

They held him … the police station.

❑ *at* ❑ *in* ❑ *on*

prallen – ***crash***

Das zweite Auto **prallte gegen** einen Baum.

The second car crashed … a tree.

❑ *against* ❑ *at* ❑ *into*

Preis – ***price, cost***

Eine ausführliche Broschüre ist erhältlich **zum Preis von** $3.

A full brochure is available … $3.

❑ *at the price of* ❑ *for price from* ❑ *to the price of*

Das müssen wir **um jeden Preis** vermeiden.

We must avoid that … all costs.

❑ *at* ❑ *by* ❑ *on*

offensichtlich to **ordnen** by **Ostern** at **passen** with **Plan** according to **Platz** in **Polizeiwache** at **prallen** into **Preis** at a price of, at

Quelle – ***source***

Diese Informationen habe ich **aus** verschiedenen **Quellen**.

I got this information … various sources.

❏ *at* ❏ *from* ❏ *out of*

Radio – ***radio***

Das habe ich **im Radio** gehört.

I heard it … the radio.

❏ *at* ❏ *in* ❏ *on*

Rat – ***advice***

Das habe ich **auf Ihren Rat hin** getan.

I did it … your advice.

❏ *from* ❏ *off* ❏ *on*

Reaktion – ***reaction***

Als **Reaktion auf** die Proteste wurde der Botschafter zurückberufen.

The ambassador was recalled as a reaction … the protests.

❏ *at* ❏ *on* ❏ *to*

Rechnung – ***bill***

Wir schicken eine **Rechnung über** den ersten Teil der Arbeiten.

We're sending a bill … the first part of the job.

❏ *across* ❏ *for* ❏ *over*

Regel – ***rule***

In der Regel gibt es keine Probleme.

… rule there are no problems.

❏ *As a* ❏ *In the* ❏ *On the*

(Rund-)Reise – ***tour***

Wir haben eine **(Rund-)Reise durch** Nordafrika vor.

We're planning a tour … North Africa.

❑ *of* ❑ *through* ❑ *to*

relevant – ***relevant***

Diese Frage ist nicht **relevant für** uns.

This question is not relevant … us.

❑ *at* ❑ *by* ❑ *to*

retten – ***save, rescue***

Ein paar antike Stücke konnte man **vor** den Flammen **retten**.

They managed to save a few antique pieces … the flames.

❑ *before* ❑ *from* ❑ *off*

riechen – ***smell***

Es **riecht** hier stark **nach** Knoblauch.

It smells strongly … garlic here.

❑ *after* ❑ *of* ❑ *with*

Risiko – ***risk***

Das machen sie **auf** eigenes **Risiko**.

They're doing it … their own risk.

❑ *at* ❑ *by* ❑ *on*

Quelle from **Radio** on **Rat** on **Reaktion** to **Rechnung** for
Regel As a **Reise** of **relevant** to **retten** from **riechen** of **Risiko** at

Rückgang – ***decrease***

Wie sehen einen **Rückgang an** (der Anzahl von) Direktbestellungen.
We are seeing a decrease … the number of direct orders.
❑ *about* ❑ *in* ❑ *on*

Ruhe – ***leisure***

Das wollen wir uns **in aller Ruhe** anschauen.
We're going to look at it … leisure.
❑ *at* ❑ *in* ❑ *on*

Saison – ***season***

Außerhalb der Saison finde ich es schöner hier.
I like it better here … season.
❑ *out the* ❑ *out of* ❑ *outside*

Schaden – ***damage***

Der Sturm richtete **Schäden an** vielen Gebäuden an.
The storm caused damage … many buildings.
❑ *at* ❑ *on* ❑ *to*

sich schämen – ***be ashamed***

Ich **schäme mich wegen** dir.
I'm ashamed … you.
❑ *at* ❑ *of* ❑ *on*

Scheck – ***cheque***

Er überreichte einen **Scheck über** $ 500.
He handed over a cheque … $ 500.
❑ *about* ❑ *for* ❑ *over*

Ich zahle **per Scheck.**

I'll pay … cheque.

❑ *by* ❑ *per* ❑ *with*

schlecht – ***bad***

Ich war schon immer **schlecht in** Mathe.

I've always been bad … maths.

❑ *at* ❑ *in* ❑ *with*

schmecken – ***taste***

Dieses Pizza **schmeckt nach** nichts.

This pizza doesn't taste … anything.

❑ *about* ❑ *of* ❑ *to*

schützen – ***protect***

Wir müssen die Blumen **vor** dem Frost **schützen**.

We must protect the flowers … the frost.

❑ *against* ❑ *before* ❑ *from*

See – ***lake***

Die Stadt liegt **am** Ontario**see**.

The town is … Lake Ontario.

❑ *at* ❑ *next to* ❑ *on*

Rückgang in **Ruhe** at **Saison** out of **Schaden** to **sich schämen** of **Scheck** for, by **schlecht** at **schmecken** of **schützen** from **See** on

Sehen – ***sight***

Ich kenne sie **vom Sehen.**

I know her ... sight.

❑ *at* ❑ *by* ❑ *on*

sehnen – ***long***

Ich **sehne** mich **nach** ein bisschen Sonne.

I'm longing ... a bit of sunshine.

❑ *after* ❑ *at* ❑ *for*

Sicht – ***run***

Wir werden **auf lange Sicht** größere Räume brauchen.

We're going to need larger rooms ... the long run.

❑ *in* ❑ *on* ❑ *to*

skeptisch – ***sceptical***

Ich bin **skeptisch gegenüber** dieser Entwicklung.

I'm sceptical ... this development.

❑ *at* ❑ *on* ❑ *of*

Sonnenaufgang/-untergang – ***dawn/dusk***

Es bot sich **bei Sonnenaufgang/-untergang** ein unbeschreibliches Panorama.

There was an unbelievable panorama ... sunrise/sunset.

❑ *at* ❑ *by* ❑ *on*

Spaß – ***fun***

Ich habe es nur **aus Spaß** getan.

I did it just … fun.

❏ *for* ❏ *from* ❏ *out of*

spezialisieren – ***specialise***

Sie sind **auf** Musikinstrumente **spezialisiert**.

They specialize … musical instruments.

❏ *at* ❏ *in* ❏ *on*

Stadium – ***stage***

Wir sind noch **im** Planungs**stadium**.

We're still … the planning stage.

❏ *at* ❏ *by* ❏ *on*

starren – ***stare***

Er **starrte** mich **an**.

He stared … me.

❏ *at* ❏ *on* ❏ *to*

Er **starrte** mir **hinterher**.

He stared … me.

❏ *after* ❏ *behind* ❏ *beyond*

Sehen by **sehnen** for **Sicht** in **skeptisch** of **Sonnenaufgang** at **Spaß** for **spezialisieren** in **Stadium** at **starren** at, after

sterben – ***die***

Sie ist **an** Krebs **gestorben**.

She died … cancer.

❑ *of* ❑ *off* ❑ *on*

Stimme – ***voice***

Mit lauter **Stimme** forderte er alle auf, sich zu erheben.

… a loud voice he called on everyone to get up.

❑ *By* ❑ *In* ❑ *Under*

stimmen – ***vote***

Sie **stimmten mit** 7 zu 4 für das Projekt.

They voted in favour of the project … 7 votes to 4.

❑ *by* ❑ *from* ❑ *with*

stolz – ***proud***

Er war sehr **stolz auf** sie.

He was very proud … her.

❑ *in* ❑ *of* ❑ *on*

Strand – ***beach***

Die Kinder waren den ganzen Tag **am Strand**.

The children were … the beach all day.

❑ *in* ❑ *on* ❑ *to*

Straße – ***street***

Wir sind uns **auf der Straße** begegnet.

We met … the street.

❑ *across* ❑ *at* ❑ *in*

Streit – ***quarrel***

Sie hat ihn **bei** einem **Streit** angespukt.

She spat at him … a quarrel.

❑ *by* ❑ *in* ❑ *on*

Stück – ***play***

Nenn mir ein **Stück von** Shakespeare.

Name a play … Shakespeare.

❑ *by* ❑ *from* ❑ *through*

Suche – ***search***

Er ist (weggegangen) **auf der Suche nach** einem Zeitungsladen.

He went off … a newsagent's.

❑ *in the look for* ❑ *in search of* ❑ *on the look for*

süchtig – ***addicted***

Er ist **nach** dieser Sendung richtig **süchtig**.

He's really addicted … this programme.

❑ *at* ❑ *on* ❑ *to*

sterben of **Stimme** In **stimmen** by **stolz** of **Strand** on **Straße** in **Streit** in **Stück** by **Suche** in search of **süchtig** to

Test

Übersetzen Sie das Deutsche ins Englische.

1. I heard it (*im Radio*) ______________________.
2. He's (*schlecht in*) ______________________ maths, but his languages are very good.
3. I only said it like that (*aus Spaß*)______________________.
4. We're going to France (*zu Ostern*)______________________.
5. We (*sind spezialisiert auf*) ______________________ leather imports.
6. They've sent a (*Rechnung über*) ______________________ $3500.
7. We must avoid it (*um jeden Preis*)______________________.
8. People (*starren mich an*) ______________________ when I wear it in the street.
9. I know them (*vom Sehen*) ______________________ but I don't know their names.
10. We're going on a (*Rundreise durch*) ______________________ Scotland in September.
11. This white bread (*schmeckt nach*) ______________________ nothing.
12. It was (*offensichtlich für*) ______________________ me that they'd just got out of bed.
13. He (*starb an*) ______________________ a heart attack.
14. If you do that, it is (*auf eigenes Risiko*)______________________.
15. The ruins looked magnificent (*bei Sonnenuntergang*)______________________.
16. What was their (*Reaktion auf*) ______________________ the news?
17. But we bought them (*auf Ihrem Rat hin*)______________________.
18. Can I pay (*per Euroscheck*)______________________?

19 Everything went very smoothly and (*nach Plan*)____________________.

20 I (*sehne mich nach*) ____________________a drink.

21 It (*riecht nach*) ____________________ smoke, don't you think?

22 I (*schäme mich wegen*) ____________________ what I did.

23 Everything is (*am richtigen Platz*)____________________.

24 (*In der Regel*) ____________________ there are no problems.

25 I'm very (*stolz auf*) ____________________ you.

[1]on the radio [2]bad at [3]for fun [4]at / for Easter [5]specialize / specialise in [6]bill for [7]at all costs [8]stare at me [9]by sight [10]tour of [11]tastes of [12]obvious to [13]died of [14]at your own risk [15]at sunset / dusk [16]reaction to [17]on your advice [18]by eurocheque [19]according to plan [20]am longing for [21]smells of [22]am ashamed of [23]in the right place [24]As a rule [25]proud of

3.5 Heißt es *at, on* oder etwa *to?*
Wendungen mit Präpositionen von T – Z

Wählen Sie die richtige Lösung.

Tag – *day*

Eulen schlafen **am Tag**.

Owls sleep … the day(time).

❑ *at* ❑ *by* ❑ *in*

Es sind 40 Jahre her **auf den Tag** genau.

It's 40 years ago … the day.

❑ *at* ❑ *on* ❑ *to*

tauschen – *exchange*

Ich möchte es **gegen** ein größeres Modell ein**tauschen**.

I'd like to exchange it … a larger model.

❑ *against* ❑ *for* ❑ to

teilnehmen – *take part*

Wir **nehmen** zum ersten Mal **an** dem Festival **teil**.

We're taking part … the festival for the first time.

❑ *by* ❑ *in* ❑ *on*

Telefon – *telephone*

Sie werden **am Telefon** verlangt.

You're wanted … the telephone.

❑ *at* ❑ *by* ❑ *on*

Temperatur – ***temperature***

Es fing alles **bei einer Temperatur** von 350° zu schmelzen an.

... a temperature of 350° everything began to melt.

❑ *At* ❑ *By* ❑ *In*

Tinte – ***ink***

Bitte **mit Tinte** schreiben.

Please write ... ink.

❑ *by* ❑ *in* ❑ *with*

Tisch – ***table, lunch***

Es tut mir Leid, sie ist **zu Tisch**.

I'm sorry, she's ... lunch.

❑ *at* ❑ *by* ❑ *to*

Wir saßen alle **bei Tisch**.

We were all ... table.

❑ *at* ❑ *by* ❑ *on*

Tod – ***death***

Bei seinem **Tod** ging der Besitz auf seine Töchter über.

... his death the property passed to his daughters.

❑ *By* ❑ *On* ❑ *To*

Tag in, to **tauschen** for **teilnehmen** in **Telefon** on **Temperatur** At **Tinte** in **Tisch** at, at **Tod** On

träumen – ***dream***

Er **träumte** wie viele Menschen **von** Ruhm und Reichtum.
Like many people he dreamt … fame and riches.
❑ *at* ❑ *from* ❑ *of*

trennen – ***part***

Es gibt einige Stücke, **von** denen ich mich nur schwer **trennen** kann.
There are some pieces I find it hard to part … .
❑ *from* ❑ *off* ❑ *with*

typisch – ***typical***

Diese Art von Brief ist **typisch für** ihn.
This kind of letter is typical … him.
❑ *for* ❑ *of* ❑ *with*

übernachten – ***stay the night, overnight***

Wir **übernachten bei** Freunden.
We're staying/overnighting … friends.
❑ *by* ❑ *over* ❑ *with*

übersetzen – ***translate***

Übersetzen aus dem Englischen **ins** Deutsche ist leichter als umgekehrt.
Translating … English … German is easier than the other way round.
❑ *from … into* ❑ *out of … to* ❑ *off … into*

Uhr – ***watch, clock***

Nach meiner Uhr ist es schon Mitternacht.
It's already midnight … my watch.
❑ *after* ❑ *by* ❑ *over*

umtauschen – *change*

Ich möchte den Pullover **gegen** eine andere Farbe **umtauschen**.
I'd like to change the pullover ... another colour.
❑ *against* ❑ *for* ❑ *to*

Unfall – *accident*

Er wurde **bei einem Unfall** schwer verletzt.
He was badly injured ... an accident.
❑ *at* ❑ *by* ❑ *in*

ungewöhnlich – *unusual*

Das **Ungewöhnliche an** dem Haus ist das flache Dach.
The unusual thing ... the house is the flat roof.
❑ *about* ❑ *at* ❑ *by*

Universität – *university*

Auf der Universität haben wir nur Theorie gelernt.
... university we only learned theory.
❑ *At* ❑ *By* ❑ *On*

träumen of **trennen** with **typisch** of **übernachten** with **übersetzen** from ... into **Uhr** by **umtauschen** for **Unfall** in **ungewöhnlich** about **Universität** At

verärgert – ***annoyed***

Ich war **über meinen Mann** sehr verärgert.

I was very annoyed … my husband.

❏ *from* ❏ *over* ❏ *with*

verbergen – ***conceal***

Sie hat versucht, **vor** ihrer Mutter alles zu **verbergen**.

She tried to conceal everything … her mother.

❏ *before* ❏ *for* ❏ *from*

verhaften – ***arrest***

Er wurde **wegen** Mordversuch **verhaftet**.

He was arrested … attempted murder.

❏ *because of* ❏ *for* ❏ *from*

verheiratet – ***married***

Sie ist **mit** einem Libanesen **verheiratet**.

She is married … a Lebanese man.

❏ *into* ❏ *to* ❏ *with*

Verkauf – ***sale***

Das Haus steht **zum Verkauf**.

The house is … sale.

❏ *at* ❏ *for* ❏ *up*

verlieben – ***fall in love***

Sie hat sich **in** das Haus gleich **verliebt**.

She fell in love … the house at once.

❏ *at* ❏ *to* ❏ *with*

verschwenden – ***waste***

Warum **verschwendet** er Zeit und Geld **für** sowas?
Why does he waste time and money … things like that?
❑ *by* ❑ *for* ❑ *on*

Versehen – ***mistake***

Es tut mir Leid; es geschah **aus Versehen**.
I'm sorry; it happened … mistake.
❑ *by* ❑ *from* ❑ *of*

verstecken – ***hide***

Die Schokolade müssen wir **vor** den Kindern **verstecken**.
We have to hide the chocolate … the children.
❑ *before* ❑ *for* ❑ *from*

verstehen – ***understand***

Was **verstehen** Sie **unter** „schnell"?
What do you understand … "quickly"?
❑ *by* ❑ *under* ❑ *with*

Vorteil – ***advantage***

Man ist **im Vorteil**, wenn man mit dem Rücken zum Fenster sitzt.
You're … an advantage if you sit with your back to the window.
❑ *at* ❑ *in* ❑ *with*

verärgert with **verbergen** from **verhaften** for **verheiratet** to **Verkauf** for **verlieben** with **verschwenden** on **Versehen** by **verstecken** from **verstehen** by **Vorteil** at

Wahrscheinlichkeit – ***probability***

Aller Wahrscheinlichkeit nach kommen wir erst am Samstag.

... all probability we won't be coming until Saturday.

❑ *According to* ❑ *By* ❑ *In*

Wand – ***wall***

Ein Kalender mit Bildern aus Alaska hing **an der Wand**.

A calendar with pictures of Alaska hung ... the wall.

❑ *against* ❑ *at* ❑ *on*

warnen – ***warn***

Er wurde **vor** den möglichen Risiken **gewarnt**.

He was warned ... the possible risks.

❑ *for* ❑ *of* ❑ *over*

Welt – ***world***

Es ist das größte Eisstadion **auf der Welt**.

It's the biggest ice stadium ... the world.

❑ *in* ❑ *on* ❑ *over*

Wetter – ***weather***

Sie ist **bei** jedem **Wetter** draußen.

She is outside ... all weathers.

❑ *by* ❑ *in* ❑ *with*

willen – ***sake***

Um Himmels Willen tu es nicht!

Don't do it ... heaven's sake.

❑ *by* ❑ *for* ❑ *over*

willkommen – *welcome*

Willkommen in London.
Welcome … London.
❑ *at* ❑ *in* ❑ *to*

Wort – *word*

Mit anderen Worten du glaubst ihm nicht.
… other words you don't believe him.
❑ *By* ❑ *In* ❑ *With*

Ich habe ihn **beim Wort genommen**.
I took him … his word.
❑ *at* ❑ *by* ❑ *on*

Wunsch – *desire*

Der **Wunsch nach** etwas Feinem zum Essen war sehr stark.
The desire … something nice to eat was very strong.
❑ *after* ❑ *at* ❑ *for*

Zahl – *number*

Wir waren nur wenige **an der Zahl**.
We were few … number.
❑ *at* ❑ *by* ❑ *in*

Wahrscheinlichkeit In **Wand** on **warnen** of **Welt** in **Wetter** in **willen** for **willkommen** to **Wort** In, at **Wunsch** for **Zahl** [1]in

zählen – ***count***

Zähle bis zehn und überlege dir gut, was du sagen willst.

Count … 10 and think carefully about what you want to say.

❏ *till* ❏ *to* ❏ *until*

Zeit – ***time***

Mit der Zeit werden Sie verstehen, was ich meine.

… time you'll understand what I mean.

❏ *After* ❏ *In* ❏ *Over*

Zu dieser **Zeit** wussten wir nichts von unserem Gewinn.

… the time we knew nothing about our win.

❏ *At* ❏ *By* ❏ *On*

Zeitpunkt – ***date***

Wir kommen **zu einem späteren Zeitpunkt** auf Sie zurück.

We'll get back to you … a later date.

❏ *at* ❏ *by* ❏ *on*

Ziel – ***destination***

Das Paar ist **mit unbekanntem Ziel** abgereist.

The couple have left … an unknown destination.

❏ *for* ❏ *to* ❏ *with*

zielen – ***aim***

Wir **zielen auf** eine Steigerung von 10%.

We're aiming … an increase of 10%.

❏ *for* ❏ *onto* ❏ *to*

zittern – ***tremble***

Das Kind **zitterte vor** Kälte.

The child was trembling … cold.

❑ *by* ❑ *for* ❑ *with*

zu Hause – ***at home***

Tanja ist nicht da, sie ist **bei einer Freundin**.

Tanja isn't here, she's … a friend's (house).

❑ *at* ❑ *by* ❑ *over*

Zufall – ***chance***

Ich habe es **per Zufall** entdeckt.

I discovered it … chance.

❑ *by* ❑ *per* ❑ *through*

Zug – ***train***

Wir sind **mit dem Zug** gekommen.

We came … train.

❑ *by* ❑ *by the* ❑ *in*

Zunahme – ***increase***

Wir beobachten zurzeit eine **Zunahme an** solchen Delikten.

We are seeing an increase … offences like these.

❑ *at* ❑ *in* ❑ *with*

zählen to **Zeit** In, At **Zeitpunkt** at **Ziel** for **zielen** for **zittern** with **zu Hause** at **Zufall** by **Zug** by **Zunahme** in

Korrigieren Sie die durchgestrichenen Präpositionen.

1 How many teams are taking part ~~at~~ ___________ the competition?

2 You're wanted ~~at~~ ___________ the telephone.

3 Can you translate that ~~in~~ ___________ German for me, please?

4 I hurt my knee ~~by~~ ___________ a car accident two years ago.

5 The dog was dreaming ~~from~~ ___________ mountains of sausages.

6 Many people are married ~~with~~ ___________ people they met at work.

7 Don't waste your money ~~for~~ ___________ things like that.

8 It won't be easy. I think I should warn you ~~for~~ ___________ the risks.

9 It's one of the biggest car factories ~~on~~ ___________ the world.

10 What do you understand ~~with~~ ___________ "a short period of time"?

11 Welcome ~~in~~ ___________ Bad Ems!

12 ~~By~~ ___________ her death the firm passed to her two sons.

13 Maybe there'll be another chance ~~on~~ ___________ a later date.

14 He was arrested ~~because~~ ___________ fraud *(Betrug)*.

15 Jimmie is staying the night ~~by~~ ___________ a friend's.

16 The unusual thing ~~at~~ ___________ the letter is that it is so inaccurate.

17 She didn't accept, ~~with~~ ___________ other words she said no.

18 Close your eyes and count ~~until~~ ___________ ten.

19 Can I change this ~~against~~ ___________ a larger size, please?

20 The home team is always ~~in~~ ___________ an advantage.

21 I think we should hide it ~~before~~ ___________ him.

22 Please complete the form ~~with~~ ___________ ink, not pencil.

23 We're aiming ~~to~~ ___________ a price under £20.

24 I'm sorry. It happened ~~from~~ ___________ mistake.

25 There has been a small increase ~~on~~ ___________ the number of complaints.

[1]in [2]on [3]into [4]in [5]of [6]to [7]on [8]of/about [9]in [10]by [11]to [12]On [13]at [14]for [15]at [16]about [17]in [18]to [19]for [20]at [21]from [22]in [23]for/at [24]by [25]in

Dieses Register enthält die deutschen Stichwörter von Kapitel 1 und die wichtigsten grammatikalischen Stichwörter von Kapitel 2. Die angegebenen Ziffern sind Seitenzahlen.